I'VE TRIED EVERYTHING & NOTHING WORKS

Empowering Your 12 & Under Child
to Overcome Severe Emotional &
Behavioral Challenges

A.J. MCMAHAN

CONTENTS

INTRODUCTION

Almost daily in my office I see a dedicated caregiver like you with a child who has problems they don't fully comprehend or know how to address—people who are hurting, frustrated and confused. Your child is likely very smart. That same child is sometimes wonderful and sweet, and at others a confusing, frustrating enigma. For perhaps months or even years, you have tried to help your child overcome the problems that concern you, but despite your exhaustive efforts, the situation has only worsened. You have hoped in vain that your child would outgrow the problems or at least that some method you've tried would help; but nothing has produced lasting results. Nothing has truly worked. Despite popular myths, we cannot control our children. If we could, you wouldn't be reading this book.

You likely feel a combination of frustration, confusion, worry, sadness, anger, and failure; perhaps you even feel you are at your wit's end. You want desperately to know what's wrong with your child and what to do about it, but regardless of your efforts to find answers, you still don't have them.

Your child has one or more of the following major concerns:

- Doesn't listen
- Does only what he wants to do
- Has a hard time accepting no or not getting his way
- Tests limits
- Throws tantrums
- Has trouble paying attention in school

- Acts out in school and/or in public
- Won't stop, won't be still
- Shuts down to the point that no one can get through for a time
- Focuses for hours on activities he enjoys but struggles with other responsibilities
- Is academically unmotivated; turns in work late or not at all
- Acts disrespectful
- Behaves aggressively
- Displays uncontrollable emotional outbursts
- Cries out for help, expressing that they want to be good but can't
- Acts defiant; lacks respect for authority
- Respects and listens to men more than women
- Feels remorse for bad choices, yet continues to repeat those bad choices

Children with these issues either have been or likely will be diagnosed with Autism Spectrum Disorder, ADHD, Impulse Control Disorder, Disruptive Mood Dysregulation Disorder, Oppositional Defiant Disorder or some other childhood behavior disorder. Though you may be wondering *why* your child has these problems, you may also wonder whether your child *can* get better.

You are not alone. In Little Rock, Arkansas, where I practice as a Licensed Professional Counselor and expert with children and families, I see before me almost every day caregivers with the same story about pre-teen children…*My child behaves in ways I don't understand or know how to help her change.*

My purpose for writing this book is so that we can help your child not only overcome these difficulties but also succeed beyond what you might think possible right now. God has led me through a journey of learning and discovery that has equipped me to help you and your child powerfully and effectively.

My goal is to empower you on a path of understanding why your child is struggling and to assist you in creating a Plan to help your child overcome the trouble. With help, you can develop a powerful belief both in what you're doing as a caregiver and in your child's ability to succeed. This book can help you accomplish these goals through the same proven methods I've used to help thousands of children and families overcome the most serious and troubling emotional and behavior problems.

The decisions you make now about how to move forward in light of the challenges your child is facing will set a course for either long-term success or immediate improvement but long-term disempowerment, discouragement and your child viewing herself as broken or defective. What you do now will affect your child for the rest of her life, and it is my desire to help you fight for both your child and your legacy.

This book is not for those looking for a quick fix. A quick fix does not exist; hope, answers, and solutions that will last a lifetime do. When we discuss what to do about what's wrong with your child, work the principles in this book completely and thoroughly. Your child needs to learn what he is capable of in order to build confidence and live a happy and successful life. We have the chance to help your child experience transformation; please don't miss it.

I know you can do this. I know your child can overcome tantrums, hitting, poor academic performance, disrespect, irresponsibility, emotional outbursts, trouble focusing, not listening, social challenges, shutting down and blowing up. You are the key. You always have been. I don't say this to place blame, but to empower you. You need to know that you are not a failure; you never were. You've been confused, you've been deceived, you've been blamed, you've been given information with the appearance of wisdom; but that is slowly crippling your child. Now, we can cast aside blame together and take up genuine understanding in its place. Together, we can help your child learn what she is really capable of and not only correct the problems, but build character and a powerful belief in God and himself.

If you don't have time or are unsure you are ready to see this through with an open mind and dedication, please put down the book and pick it up when you are ready. There is a time for you to read this book and absorb what God has for you. It may be now, or it may be later; but don't fail to listen to yourself and your needs. Trust God. Wait until you are ready. When you are, let's do this. Your child is worth every ounce of time and pain you will pour into helping your child achieve true success, happiness and safety. After you have experienced your hopes fulfilled, share this book with someone else. Let's change the world, together, one child at a time. Let's begin with yours.

CHAPTER 1

CONFUSION

> Truth is ever to be found in simplicity, and not in the
> multiplicity and confusion of things.
>
> —Isaac Newton

I've come to learn that one of the greatest obstacles hindering caregivers from being the most powerful force in motivating a child to do everything we hope for him is confusion. Confusion is the death of conviction and consistency. Sure, caregivers are convicted to help their child succeed, but they don't know the most beneficial answers to the following two questions: what's wrong with my child, and what do I do about it?

Loving caregivers like yourself don't want to do anything to make their child worse. They don't want to be too soft, but they don't want to be too hard either. Caregivers want to help, not hurt, their children. The problem is twofold: you've never had the opportunity to this point, first of all, to know exactly what is causing your child's problems, and secondly, to focus on what is the most effective way to help your child succeed.

When caregivers are in this confused state they change tactics, don't agree on what to do with co-caregivers and others, and are hindered in doing the Most Effective Actions on a daily basis to help their child succeed. This hindrance is enough to produce a feeling of failure. The enemy uses confusion to cripple us just enough to make us miss the mark in helping our children succeed. As long as we are confused, we can't act with conviction; and we can't be consistent about what we believe is best for our child.

I present in this book what consistently helps thousands of children and families that I have the privilege of counseling. I will begin by sharing information about why children struggle; as I do, you will likely recognize pieces of information that are at the root of why your child is struggling. I know the information presented may not be popular, but what do you have to lose? You've tried everything else, right? I'm not asking you to blindly believe what I've written. I'm asking you to open your mind to it and ask yourself if it seems to make sense with your child. You fill in the pieces about your child that I can't since I don't know your child; then together, with God's guidance, we will formulate true understanding of the core issues causing your child's difficulties.

The 70% to 80% Rule

It has been my experience that you are already doing on a daily basis at least 70% to 80% of the Most Effective Actions to help your child succeed. At this point, you likely don't believe that statement because you're not seeing success, but some things are true whether we believe them or not. Confusion has been robbing you of your true conviction and consistency, and without that, the formula needed for success has not been employed. In our work together, we will identify your 70% to 80%—and figure out how to raise that percentage even higher. The truth is caregivers are doing much better on average than they think they are and know more than they think they know. I have seen children with the most intense social, emotional, relational and behavioral problems overcome them for good once their caregivers are empowered with the right information. Your child's problems are complex and may have raged for years, but we will take your concerns seriously and work through them together.

The right information is not a list of do's and don'ts. Most caregivers, like the ones that come into my office, need something more when children are throwing tantrums, acting out in public, displaying irresponsible behavior, not listening, hitting, shutting down, repeating themselves, whining, crying and not doing their work. In these situations, conventional wisdom has failed. Many children are already on psychotropic medication or caregivers are seriously considering using them because they are desperate to help their child turn their problems around.

Remember I said that you are probably doing at least 70% to 80% of the Most Effective Actions on a daily basis to help your child succeed? Unfortunately, this is not enough. Our responsibility as caregivers is to give our children the best chance to succeed. In order to do so, we must operate consistently in the 97% to 98% range of the Most Effective Actions on a daily basis. This is the path to empowerment of a child—a path we can believe in.

When caregivers are empowered in a way they believe in, this is a huge part of operating in that 97% to 98% range. I've seen consistently and almost without fail that caregivers operating in the context of a loving relationship with the child, working to do 97% to 98% of the Most Effective Actions on a daily basis to help their child succeed, are the ones who assist their child in achieving lasting transformations.

Let's be clear. Some of you do not necessarily feel love for the child in your care. That's okay. The love of God is not a feeling. It is a sacrifice. If you are willing to sacrifice for the child you're trying to help, regardless of how you might feel, that is love.

What I have seen time and time again with my very own eyes is that when caregivers operate in the 97% to 98% range of the Most Effective Actions on a daily basis based on the understanding and empowerment offered in this book, their children change. Caregivers operate in a way they believe in, trusting in God, themselves and even in the potential of their child...and those children reach their potential. They thrive. They are happier than ever and successful.

I'm going to challenge you now to have faith, to choose hope, to embrace love, not as a feeling but as choice. Let me share with you real-life stories using pseudonyms of families who have taken the LEAP (L.E.A.P.) to conquer despair. What is L.E.A.P.? L.E.A.P. brings together all that you have to help you bring out all God intends in you and your child. Stay connected. We will take the L.E.A.P. together as soon as possible. First, faith and hope.

REAL-LIFE STORIES

I've seen empowered caregivers, through a loving relationship with their child, identify and begin to practice consistently 97% to 98% of the Most Effective Actions on a daily basis. Their children have been empowered to achieve lasting transformations. Grant, Jasmine, Devan, Mia and Phil are pseudonyms for a few of these children. Their stories began like this:

Grant – Age 7

Grant's caregivers were not together but were excellent co-caregivers. Grant was a bright boy, empathetic at times and a wonderful kid; however, Grant's caregivers were at the end of their rope. Grant was a highly impulsive child, diagnosed with ADHD around the age of five. He would "bounce off the walls" constantly. During the school day, when he was on ADHD medication, he behaved well; however, mornings before he took his medication and evenings after school with no medication were a horror. Grant would hit his mother and was a terror to put to bed at night. His caregivers disciplined him when he behaved badly, which stopped the bad behavior momentarily, but never for long. Grant's caregivers hated threatening to punish him all the time and wished he would listen and do what he was told.

Jasmine – Age 5

Jasmine started her pre-K4 program and began throwing temper tantrums about two weeks into the program, though Jasmine had never thrown any temper tantrums at home. Jasmine's mom was called by the school when she had tantrums, and Jasmine would hate talking to her mom on the phone about her disruptive behavior. When her mom scolded her, Jasmine was contrite, cried a little and did what she was supposed to do for the rest of the day; however, Jasmine continued to throw tantrums in school. Her mom would discipline her appropriately at home for throwing tantrums. Despite Jasmine's mom addressing her behavior consistently, Jasmine got worse instead of better. For the rest of the school year, Jasmine's mom had a call from the school on almost a daily basis. No matter how much Jasmine's mom talked, prayed, cried, begged, pleaded, reminded, threatened, disciplined and/or rewarded, Jasmine continued to throw tantrums in school almost every day the entire school year.

Phil – Age 8

Phil was brought to my office by a couple who was planning to adopt him later that year. Phil had significant problems in school and at home with lack of focus. Phil struggled to concentrate at school, on homework and follow through with tasks. At times, these struggles led to emotional and behavioral outbursts, primarily at home. When Phil took his medication, he focused much better in school and on homework, and also demonstrated greater ability to follow through with tasks. Phil's foster caregivers brought him to me near the end of his third-grade school year. They were planning on adopting him that summer and wanted him to have support through the adjustment. His foster caregivers also wanted him assessed again for ADHD since he had been diagnosed with it and was on medication for it. Phil's foster caregivers adopted him that summer. They wanted him off medication, but with Phil's difficulties focusing, following through with tasks and sometimes displaying outbursts when not on his medication, they were concerned that he would fail or struggle without it.

Mia – Age 9

Mia was the "stormy twin." Her behavior was the "night" to her twin sister's "day." For seven of the nine years of her life, Mia's caregivers witnessed her meltdowns. Uncontrollable, inconsolable crying spells caused her caregivers to believe that maybe Mia was broken in some way. No amount of love, attention, discipline or yelling helped Mia. Her sister never had problems listening or with tantrums. Mia was a whole different story.

Devan

Devan had epileptic seizures. He also had emotional, social, academic and behavioral problems. Devan had trouble doing what he was told, following through with tasks, and was aggressive to his peers and siblings. His caregivers were extremely confused as to which or to what degree Devan's problems were influenced by neurological issues.

These are stories about actual children that have experienced life-altering empowerment. Grant, Jasmine, Phil, Mia and Devan's caregivers are a microcosm of millions of loving and dedicated, albeit confused, caregivers. These caregivers love these children. As in Phil's case, a caregiver doesn't have to be a biological parent to truly want the best for the child. These five children and so many others have experienced transformations. It's time for your child as well.

Many caregivers are like Jasmine and Grant's caregivers, at their wit's end after having tried everything to no avail. Caregivers often feel concerned, frustrated, angry, fearful and like they are failures. Grant and Jasmine's caregivers were not failures, and neither are you. We caregivers struggle. You are not alone. Hearing "caregiving is hard" is not the half of it. If you met Grant, Jasmine, Phil, Mia and Devan today, you would never believe they ever had the problems they once had. Their families are happy and excited to see their children thrive.

These families are happy because they were given the opportunity to look beyond disorders and see what their children were capable of. If your child has been diagnosed with a disorder like ADHD or Autism Spectrum Disorder primarily due to behavior concerns, I'm not saying that the diagnosis of the symptoms he is displaying do not apply. I am also not anti-medication. What I am against is the belief that children are defective and that they can't overcome the symptoms they are displaying. They can and often do when we empower them to do so.

When I helped Jasmine's mom clear the confusion by helping her understand exactly what was going on with Jasmine, why she was acting out and what she could do about it—the same information I'm sharing in this book—Jasmine's mom got onboard, albeit reluctantly. She was skeptical that just tweaking what she was already doing, moving from that 70% to 80% of the Most Effective Actions on a daily basis to help Jasmine succeed to the 97% to 98% range, would help Jasmine make such an amazing turnaround; but it did. This happened for Grant, Jasmine, Phil, Mia, Devan and countless others. Regardless of the problems, regardless of the diagnosis, it is possible to help children overcome the struggles they are having. The power is inside each of you. This book will help you unlock that power.

There is tremendous hope for your child. What I offer you is truth and hard work. I wish I had a fast, easy answer for the struggles your child is facing. I wish mere tips and tricks would help your child out of the mess she is in. They won't. What I offer you is truth about why our children are struggling. Much of what I write will not be popular, but it is very likely what you need to hear. Despite our popular theories about treating ADHD, autism and other childhood problems, the rates of these problems are skyrocketing, not decreasing. If we in the medical profession, especially counselors, are really doing our jobs well, we should be trying to put ourselves out of business. If me being out of business means children will be happy, successful and safe, the cost will be worth it.

First, I'm going to share my journey. I want you to see how I got to the place where I ended up writing this book. I want you to see the passion I have for your child to succeed. Then we will tackle some theories for you to consider concerning what may be behind your child's problems. Later, we will go into more detail about some of the real life stories shared earlier. My hope is that you will open your mind to possibilities you might never have considered before and thus remove the confusion that prevents you from working to empower your child. You can't take anyone further than you've gone yourself. I hope to first empower you; then, when you are ready to make practical application of the information, I'll walk you through steps to take the L.E.A.P. Our goal is not better behavior; it's solid building. We will empower your child to build internal skills that will provide confidence, an awesome sense of self and change that will last a lifetime.

My Story

I was raised by a single mother, Mildred. My dad left when I was six and never returned. My mom was not perfect. She worked a lot and had little time to spend with me. As a result, our bond was tenuous at best. Mom was a firm disciplinarian, yet I knew she loved me.

The world assigns responsibility to caregivers for their child's actions, so I guess it was my mom's fault that I accidentally burned down a university storage shed while playing with matches, shoplifted, lied, stole and spent a few hours in jail, all by the time I was 12.

My mom wasn't a bad mother or a failure. True, she didn't spend enough time with me, and I certainly didn't have enough supervision; but she loved me. (Just as I did, your child is acting in ways you didn't teach or model. Kids struggle. God wants you to stop blaming yourself, and others for that matter, for your child's challenges.)

Fast forward to my life 13 years later. I received a graduate degree in Marriage and Family Therapy from Harding University in 1998 and began my career as a licensed counselor. After more than 20 years in the field and a great deal of trial and error, here I am.

Harmony of My Personal & Professional Journeys

As I look back over my professional career path and see the extensive opportunities God has given me to work with youth and families; I know that there has been a divine purpose for my journey. During the first nine years of my professional career, I had the privilege of counseling troubled youth in an alternative school, a residential treatment center, a juvenile detention center and a center for families struggling to overcome the horrors of domestic violence.

After nine years of working in the field of counseling, I was invited to join the private practice of a renowned child and adolescent psychiatrist who had been working in the field for 30 plus years when he invited me in and poured his wisdom and experience into me. We spent countless hours studying together and refining our craft.

This psychiatrist prided himself on having a stable practice. In fact, he had the exact same office for most of his 30 plus years (which was fairly evident by the carpet wall covering *circa* 1970). Working exclusively with patients 18 and under and their families during the 7 years that I worked at this office allowed me to focus on how to help this age group succeed. Being in this one practice with stable patient relationships over time was a rare opportunity to see young people at various points in their development. Caregivers brought children to us who were struggling with behavior problems in school, at home and at daycare. Children presented with anxiety, aggressive outbursts, destructive behavior, not listening, running away from home, inattention, lack of motivation, tantrums, defiance, social issues, depression and behaving in ways that threatened their futures.

Most caregivers were in dire straits when they came to us, and my desire was to help.

I found most caregivers to be dedicated, hardworking and very involved with their children. These adults had literally tried everything they could think of or were prescribed to do to help their children overcome the problems; however, the issues only grew worse.

As humans, we are geared to ask and want to understand why a problem is occurring. When our children have emotional, social and/or behavioral problems, we caregivers typically want to know why, even if those answers are difficult. For treatment purposes, understanding the contributing factors to a patient's problems allows us to help the patient work through those issues. If any contributing factors are ongoing, it's often important to resolve them.

It is widely believed in the field of psychology that the reasons children have emotional and behavioral disturbances are due to some force beyond their control such as, but not limited to:

- Brain dysfunction
- Genetic disposition
- Poor caregiving
- Issues in utero
- Developmental disorders
- Bullying
- Teachers and administrators dropping the ball
- Trauma

However, the vast majority of children I've worked with, including those displaying even the most severe emotional, behavioral and academic struggles, had none of these as a primary contributing factor to their problems. What then, you might wonder, is likely at the root of your child's struggles? Let me share what I've found time and time again to be the answer to the caregiver's most pressing question: "What's wrong with my child?"

CHAPTER 2

WHAT'S WRONG WITH MY CHILD?

"If you continue to believe your child is broken, you are lost and so is your child."

—AJ McMahan

One of the main reasons caregivers today are not effective in helping their child overcome their problems is that the caregiver is confused about what is wrong with their child and what to do about it. When caregivers seek to understand what is causing their child's problems they find conflicting information and/or recommendations with the appearance of wisdom. Many caregivers instinctively struggle with following these recommendations because something tells them what they're being told is not quite right. In addition, even when following recommendations from family, resources, professionals and others, their child's struggles continue to manifest.

Caregivers are pouring a ton of energy into helping their children succeed, but they are either misdirected, misinformed, or undermined in their processes. These factors cause caregivers to miss the mark when it comes to empowering their child to succeed. Misdirection, misinformation and undermining are all tools of the enemy to hinder our ability to help our children reach their potential.

As a professional, I was tacitly, and at times directly, taught that faulty caregiving lies at the root of children having problems with their emotions and behavior. Over time, my experience as both a caregiver and a child and family therapist provided mounting evidence to refute this widely held belief. Like the movie "Groundhog Day," I repeatedly encountered caregivers who were working hard and acting effectively to help their children succeed; however, their children were not successful. As my understanding of what causes children to struggle with emotional, social and behavioral difficulties grew, the more I realized the gross error in thinking when it comes to judging caregivers of kids with challenging issues.

If it's not faulty caregiving, then the other "usual suspects" to explain a child's confusing and problematic behavior are typically a traumatic antecedent, a significant life factor such as bullying, video games and/or media. During my work, detailed exploration into each client's life and history ruled out these factors time and time again as the root causes of the present problems the children were experiencing. Often, the only things left as a potential root cause were either brain disorders or genetics.

Many factors supported the brain disorder theory, including neurodevelopmental disorders, but the closer I examined, the more conflicting evidence I found both in research and the daily life of the families I worked with. My professional search for the root causes of children's problematic emotions and behavior led me to the information I'm going to share with you. The three primary factors most powerfully influencing the problems your child is having are brain development/neuroscience, internal temperament and environment.

Misdirection, Misinformation and Undermining

Our spiritual enemy is real with the goal of undermining the love and power of God. Waging war on the family is foundational to long-term undermining the effect that God's love and power manifest in our lives.

Our children need us to choose true wisdom and embrace faith in order to avoid being unintentional pawns in the enemy's game.

Much of what is becoming popular theory regarding what is wrong with our children and what to do about it has the appearance of wisdom, yet perniciously undermines the fabric of our children's potential, confidence and well-being. We are being taught kids are disordered instead of understanding the truth of their development. Lovingly firm discipline is being presented as being unhealthy, when in fact it is a powerful and effective extension of love. Caregivers are led to believe something is wrong with their child when they don't do what they "should" do instead of understanding the naturally occurring factors within their child and his own internal world that causes these discrepancies to make sense.

God wants us to have the truth and experience the freedom of it. God wants us to see clearly where our children are instead of our vision being distorted by where we are led to believe they "should" be. I've seen time and time again that caregivers armed with the right information about what's going on with their child have a much easier time understanding what to do to truly help their child succeed.

The first thing we want to do is move you from misinformation to truth, from misdirection to a path of victory, from undermining to empowerment. Open your mind and your heart as we discuss the following truths with courage. My great hope is that we will embrace and use God's truths about our kids to help your child get better once and for all.

In the next chapter, we will dive right into one of the most popular and erroneous weapons of the enemy to disempower our kids...the belief that they are disordered.

CHAPTER 3

BRAIN DEVELOPMENT/ NEUROSCIENCE

Dysfunctional Brain? What About the Developing Brain?

Imagine that your child is working on a project in school. Your child's teacher came by when your child was 45% into developing her project. Upon viewing the project, the teacher stated, "Your project is a mess." The teacher then examined the project further, testing its functionality and said, "Your project doesn't work right. Fix this or you will get a bad grade." How might you respond to this teacher? How might you feel about this evaluation of your child and her project in the midst of its development? Would it be fair for the teacher to make these comments when your child's project is only 45% complete? Of course it wouldn't. Then why do the world's teachers critique our children's brains in this way?

Science has been revealing that a person's brain is not fully developed until late adolescence or even early adulthood. In the October 2011 edition of *National Geographic Magazine,* in the article "Beautiful Brains" written to highlight teens' brains related to why teenagers act the way they do, author David Dobbs writes about the developing, maturing brain:

> This process of maturation, once thought to be largely finished by elementary school, continues throughout adolescence. Imaging work done since the 1990s shows that

> these physical changes move in a slow wave from the brain's rear to its front, from areas close to the brain stem that look after older more behaviorally basic functions, such as vision, movement and fundamental processing, to the evolutionary newer and more complicated thinking areas up front. (pg. 43)

By the age of 5, your child's brain size and structure are 90% developed; however, science has revealed that your child's developmental functioning of his brain still has a long way to go.

Since the late 1980s and early 1990s, science has begun to reveal the true developmental process of our brains. The frontal lobe of our brain, responsible for executive functioning including judgment, impulse control and emotional regulation, does not fully mature until a person is a young adult. Does your child struggle with impulse control? What about emotional control? How about judgment? The article further shares:

> Self-regulation has been broadly classified as the management of emotions and motivation. Self-regulation also entails controlling the expression of intense emotions, impulse control and delayed gratification. As adolescents progress toward adulthood with a body that is almost mature, the self-regulatory parts of their brains are still maturing. Behavioral control requires a great involvement of cognitive and executive functions. These functions are localized in the prefrontal cortex, which matures independent of puberty and continues to evolve up until 24 years of age.

> (Arain, Mariam, et al. "Maturation of the Adolescent Brain." Neuropsychiatric Disease and Treatment, Dove Medical Press, 3 Apr. 2013, www.ncbi.nlm.nih.gov/pmc/articles/PMC3621648/.)

For your child age 12 and under, the executive functioning center of the brain, the frontal lobe, which is responsible for impulse control, judgment and the management of emotions, is not the part of the brain in charge. The most dominant parts of his brain are responsible for impulses, instincts, emotions and reactions.

We will see later, if this is the case for all children developmentally, what causes children to behave so differently. For now, I want to shed light on the ever-growing, yet mostly erroneous, theory that your child's brain is dysfunctional when, in fact, it is still under major construction.

Something that may help provide insight is our frustrating friend, the flat tire. Have you ever experienced or dealt with a flat tire? Flats are aggravating. When someone has a flat tire, the tire has been deflated. When a tire is truly flat, the surface on which the tire is placed will not determine its condition. Let's say you put the tire on a concrete surface. Would the tire still be flat? Yes. What about asphalt? Of course. Dirt? Gravel?...right, still flat. A flat tire is flat regardless of surface.

Think about that in connection to your child's troubles. Do your child's problems exist regardless of the day, time, place, person, or situation? A flat tire is consistently flat; however, I often see children who are "flat" in one location (situation) but not in others. A flat tire is flat in every context. So if your child's problem is truly a brain disorder or genetic, how do the problems turn on and turn off...consistently?

When I began to take a step back from the popular theories of childhood disorders, I began to recognize patterns in the behavior of almost 100% of the children with whom I worked. These patterns show up as inconsistencies in the struggles they are having. Kids will display terrible tantrums at school but not at home and vice versa. They will listen better to males than females, listen to coaches but not caregivers, some days do what they are told and other days they cannot. A child will not be able to focus for long with schoolwork or chores but spend the entire day hyper-focusing on a video game. A child who cannot remember to do his daily chore seems to never forget anything you promise him.

If your child's brain is broken, how can there be such patterns to the problems? Trust me, a dysfunction of the brain cannot "pick and choose." If a problem with the brain causes poor focus, how can the brain focus for long periods of time with consistent results in just some areas but not others? If a child cannot control herself, how can she exhibit control sometimes and in pattern? If a brain is broken, it is broken. From my experience, there is a greater chance than not that your child's brain is not broken, damaged or defective.

Our children are smart. They *know* right from wrong, just like we adults do; but unlike adults, they do not have the executive functioning skills that we do to consistently choose right over wrong. Ever had your child say something like, "I want to do good, but I just can't help myself." Or, "I try to do good, but I just can't." or "Mommy, I'm bad"? If you've heard your child, aged 12 and under, proclaim some variation of this truth, particularly with great emotion, that child is not typically making a statement related to her self-esteem. In these moments, your child is simply yet profoundly communicating the truth she experiences: "I cannot carry out choosing to do what's right consistently, in and of myself."

God designed it so that we are to act as pseudo-frontal lobes for our children, aged 12 and under, until theirs are fully developed.

> *Train up a child in the way he should go, And when he is old*
> *he will not depart from it.*
>
> —Proverbs 22:6, NKJV

Notice the verse reads, "and when he is old." Your young child is not developmentally equipped to display the good behavior and the amazing self you see at times in and of himself. When belief in brain dysfunctions cause us to doubt our child's capability, we lower the bar for him, which unintentionally robs him of confidence and success. When we understand our children in the light of development, we can understand why they seem governed by emotions, impulses and reactions...because children 12 and under, by the light of neuroscience, are.

This truth of your child's fundamental need for support to consistently make good choices outside of herself gives credence for psychotropic medication. Psychotropic medication powers children to focus, behave, calm down and make better choices. The problem is that although psychotropic medication powers children, it does not empower children. The difference between *powers* and *empowers* is so unnoticeable behaviorally, but there is a fundamentally wide chasm between the two. The children of caregivers who take it upon themselves to understand and act on the difference have the greatest potential to avoid falling into that chasm in the long run. When we operate in line with the popular theories of childhood brain disorders, we do not and cannot believe a child is fully capable of overcoming specific problems. The underlying doubt in our child's ability to succeed is one of the greatest self-fulfilling prophecies of childhood disorders.

Psychotropic meds can decrease symptoms for a time. If your child has been or currently is on psychotropic meds, that was likely a tough decision to begin with. Using meds for a time to help your child is nothing to feel bad about at all, in my opinion. The important thing is knowing the truth: that we have to help your child build the skills to overcome the problem, or your child will just become worse in the long run developmentally, even if the behavior is better in the short term.

Furthermore, when did God start abandoning children's brains in the creation process?

> *For you created my inmost being; you knit me together in my mother's womb. I praise you because I am fearfully and wonderfully made; your works are wonderful, I know that full well.*
>
> —Psalm 139:13-14

Did God decide to put down knitting to take up basket weaving? Fishing perhaps? Jesus fished, didn't He? Did God start abandoning brains, sparking the epidemic known as ADHD? I don't think so. We do not typically assess something incomplete as dysfunctional. We do not look at anything being built and criticize it for not functioning the way the completed project will, except with the most complicated machine of them all...our human brains. Your child's brain is more than likely not dysfunctional...it is developing.

So if every child 12 and under has a developing brain in which the executive functioning center responsible for controlling emotions, reactions and impulses is not the part of the brain primarily in charge, why do some children behave so well and others do not? We answer this by understanding the true internal motivations of children prominently driving the way they interact with the world through their own internal temperament.

CHAPTER 4

INTERNAL TEMPERAMENTAL AFFINITY

Inner Temperament: What Is It?

Sometimes your child acts like the sweet, loving and respectful child that you know he is, and at other times he acts completely the opposite. Many caregivers share that it's like a "switch flips" with their child. The capriciousness you witness in your child is not bipolar disorder. Your child is also not displaying the results of genetics when his behavior resembles a family member that acts the same way. The back-and-forth struggle your child has emotionally and behaviorally, the essence of Dr. Jekyll and Mr. Hyde, is your child's battle between life and temperament.

Temperament describes a child's innate way of operating with her world. Inner temperament uncovers powerful yet hidden influences in the motivation and thus the behavior of our children. When a child's behavior seems so unnatural, we look for extraordinary causes to explain what doesn't make sense. This has been happening for decades.

Around the 1950s, environment was touted as one of the most prominent core issues related to children's extreme and problematic behavior, yet there were gross inconsistencies. Dr. Alexander Thomas, child psychiatrist; Dr. Stella Chess, child development specialist; and Dr. Herbert G.

Birch, professor of pediatrics at the Albert Einstein College of Medicine in New York were among those who recognized and wanted to understand the common discrepancies between a child's behavior problems and her environment. In order to do so, they launched the New York Longitudinal Study (NYLS).

The NYLS started in 1956 and spanned several decades; it is regarded as a classic study into personality types and temperament traits. Dr. Alexander Thomas, Dr. Stella Chess and Dr. Herbert G. Birch were principal contributors in their search to understand the dichotomies between a child's behavior and environment. In 1970, Chess, Thomas and Birch published findings from their study in the *Scientific American* magazine. Here's what they discovered:

> As physicians who have frequent occasion to examine the family background of disturbed children, we began many years ago to encounter reasons to question the prevailing one-sided emphasis on environment. We found that some children with severe psychological problems had a family upbringing that did not differ essentially from the environment of other children who developed no severe problems. On the other hand, some children were found to be free of serious personality disturbances although they had experienced severe family disorganizations and poor parental care. Such unpredictability seemed to be the direct consequence of omitting an important factor from the evaluation: the child's own temperament, that is, his own individual style of responding to the environment. It is our hypothesis that personality is shaped by the constant interplay of temperament and environment.

What doctors Chess, Thomas and Birch found helps us with an important piece of the puzzle concerning our children: innate temperament.

The NYLS found that most children in their study had one of three temperaments as their primary or dominate inner temperament. They are:

1. Easy/compliant
2. Slow to warm up
3. Difficult or "strong-willed" (term used by Dr. James Dobson)

Inner temperament is how each child is internally motivated to interact with his world and authority—"the boss." I've discovered that:

- Compliant children **want to please the boss.**
- Slow-to-warm-up children **don't want to upset the boss.**
- Strong-willed children **want to be the boss.**

Compliant, "easy" children are strongly motivated from within, just like slow-to-warm-up or strong-willed, difficult children. It just so happens that children operating with the compliant temperament are internally motivated to please others, achieve and receive approval, which easily fits our expectations and societal norms. Children operating with a compliant temperament don't struggle much when it comes to doing what they are supposed to do. Compliant children struggle with the idea of not pleasing someone and with perfectionism. A compliant child's internal struggles lead to quiet battles with anxiety and depression. These struggles for the compliant child are not caused by caregivers, but are a function of how the compliant child interacts with her world. Children who are slow to warm up don't want to make waves or be in the spotlight. They are often more sensitive to the feelings and needs of others. These children can also wrestle with anxiety when they sense anxiety in those around them. They can be easily overlooked in the maelstrom of a family dealing with a challenged child, sometimes self-sufficiently drifting to the background to avoid putting a further burden on a family already emotionally, physically and mentally weighed down.

Just like the compliant child's strength is responsibility and the slow-to-warm-up child's strength is self-sufficiency, the strong-willed child's strength is independence. The unrefined strength of the strong-willed child's internal temperament manifests in various external battles including not listening, not following through with tasks, outbursts, shutting down, aggression, destructiveness, lack of responsibility, helplessness, trouble focusing and what seems to be anxiety, to name some but not all of the major issues.

The following are common characteristics of each of the three inner temperaments:

Compliant, "Easy" Children:

- Follow the rules well
- Want to please and achieve
- Get frustrated when others are not following the rules
- Are prone to internal struggles with anxiousness
- Can be overly responsible for themselves and others
- Struggle with perfectionism
- Fight for high achievement
- Become bossy when others are not being compliant

Slow-to-Warm-Up Children:

- Hate making waves
- Take a while to warm up socially; interact well once warmed up
- Don't like the spotlight
- Are extremely perceptive to the feelings and emotions of others
- Can go unnoticed

- Can be extremely self-sufficient
- Need to go at their own pace
- Are susceptible to anxiety by becoming emotionally overburdened
- Can be misdiagnosed as depressed or oppositional after extended periods of operating self-sufficiently

Strong-Willed or "Difficult" Children:

- Want life on their terms
- Are extremely bright
- Use their intelligence to live life on their terms
- Want others to do what they want or play how they want to play
- Get frustrated when they have to do what they don't want to do
- Lack motivation concerning what they "should" do
- Are susceptible to anxiety related to their choices
- March to the beat of their own drum
- Manifest most of their struggles externally

The temperamental affinity with which a child is dominantly operating drives the child from within. Compliant children appear to have more developed executive functioning skills because they are internally motivated to please the boss. This is similarly true of slow-to-warm-up children who don't want to upset the boss. When a child is internally driven to be the boss, however, the way he interacts with his world is quite different. These interactions can manifest from anxiety to tantrums, yet the hidden internal motivation is the same—to do what he wants and get out of doing what he doesn't want to do. Temperament can be shaped just like personality. You may notice your child operating in line with more than one temperament. This is normal as children are meant to develop the strengths of all three.

Inner Temperament: Why It's Important

When we understand the true role inner temperament plays, many previously confusing factors will begin to make sense. Ever wonder why kids basically raised in the same way can act so differently? Why reward charts work with some kids and fail with others? Why your child is not motivated to do what he "should" do? Why your exhaustive efforts to understand what's wrong with your child and what to do about it have fallen short? These are all affected by the power of inner temperament.

Your child's behavior can seem chaotic or random and be confusing; however, to your child, his behavior and the problems that result make sense. Let's revisit these words from the New York Longitudinal Study:

> Such unpredictability seemed to be the direct consequence of omitting an important factor from the evaluation: the child's own temperament, that is, his own individual style of responding to the environment. It is our hypothesis that personality is shaped by the constant interplay of temperament and environment.

Regardless of how you've witnessed your child respond to her world, it is extremely unlikely that she is disordered, out of control, or a sociopath. Adult caregivers and professionals often look at children from the view of where we are trying to groom them to be, or in light of how they "should act," not developmentally where they are. As adults, we have brains with a mostly or fully developed executive functioning center, developed character in relation to self-discipline and self-control, developed moral compasses, and God-given wisdom from life experience. Our children are developing these, yet have a long way to go. What primarily drives children 12 and under are impulses and temperament.

The most dominant parts of a child's brain 12 years and younger are the parts responsible for impulses, reactions and emotions. The brain development of the typical compliant, strong-willed or slow-to-warm-up child, age 12 and under, is relatively the same; however, her internally driven motivations are significantly different. For compliant children, the reward is in pleasing. For slow-to-warm-up children, the reward is in not making waves. Children operating in line with the strong-willed temperament reap the rewards of having life on their terms in whatever forms work best for them.

If we could control our children, you wouldn't be reading this book. We know our children have God-given free will. We also must understand our children have their own personal internally driven motivations while also being influenced, but not controlled by, external factors. The outcry of the strong-willed temperament is to have life on its terms; however, the manifestations of internal temperament are various, much more subtle, and extremely powerful.

Temperament & Energy

Our children's internal motivations direct their flow of energy. Children operating with the compliant temperament direct their energy into choices that will bring them approval and please others. Compliant children are responsible, motivated to achieve and typically work hard. They push their energy into following the rules because the rewards of approval are powerful to them. It's no wonder that children operating with the compliant temperament as dominant are called "easy children."

Children operating with the slow-to-warm-up temperament direct their energy away from upsetting others. They also direct their energy into being cautious, assessing and moving into situations at their own pace. Slow-to-warm-up children typically direct their energy away from the spotlight and into caring for others due to their sensitivity to others' feelings. Sometimes this means using their energy to take care of themselves to free up caregivers to direct their energy elsewhere.

When a child operates in line with the strong-willed temperament, his energy is directed into living life on his terms. When we discuss a child motivated internally to have life on his terms, to have what he wants and get out of what he doesn't want, this will resonate with many of you. Some of you know that your strong-willed child wants her way and has problems when she doesn't get her way.

We also need to understand that there are many more situations where the role of temperament is not so easily distinguished. These caregivers feel that their child is anxious, has trouble focusing that is beyond his control, is acting almost exactly the same as a particular adult in his family, or perhaps has been influenced by a trauma. The problem is that, despite efforts to quantify, understand and support that child according to best practices with these struggles, the child is not improving significantly and consistently.

Children are discovering life. Sometimes they discover a way that makes life more interesting, fun, comfortable, easier, or powerful to them. The immediate gratification of having aspects of their lives play out in these ways becomes enticing to many children. Then children become driven from within to continue to experience life in these ways. The problem is that what is often maladaptive for a child's life is often adaptive to him personally.

When Johnny throws a tantrum, this behavior is likely more in line with his feelings, internal motivation and impulses. It is actually more normal and rewarding to Johnny to throw the tantrum than to not throw the tantrum. If Johnny throws the tantrum, here are all the potential outcomes that could be pleasing to him:

- Releasing his emotions in an immediately gratifying way
- Getting out of what he doesn't want to do
- Others capitulating
- Lessening of responsibility
- The possibility of getting his way

What would be motivating factors for him to control himself?

- It's the right thing to do.
- He wants to avoid trouble.
- He promised he would do better.
- He doesn't want to upset/hurt others.

In the moment of challenge, despite the remorse afterward, the power of the influence of the first list will most often outweigh the power of the second list. This is what causes Johnny to give in to his impulses and throw a tantrum time and time again.

What about children who don't focus well or follow through with tasks? We want them to pour their energy into tasks they find difficult, boring, or don't really care about. Just because a child "should" care about something doesn't mean he does. The child in those moments seek escape from the undesirable task. Escape can be in the form of daydreaming and/or finding something else more enjoyable to do. This is when caregivers find their child either zoned out or playing around when he should be doing something specific.

At times, escape can be outbursts of "I can't" and "I'm stupid" or needing someone to be right there with him the whole time. The latter eases the burden of the activity for the child. Sometimes escape is shutting down. Your child is smart, right? Smart enough not to tell you to your face, "I'm not gonna." When caregivers get confused about what is going on and think the problem is related to something beyond the child's control, the child's maladaptive response to the situation is reinforced.

Children pour energy into activities that are rewarding and stimulating to them. We explain away these choices as "hyperfocusing" and the like when the truth is related to what your child is motivated to pour her energy into and what she is not motivated to pour her energy into. Recognize that compliant children pour energy into responsible behavior because the potential outcomes are rewarding to them. What about the millions of children who do not find "pleasing the boss" personally rewarding? What do they find in their lives to be stimulating, rewarding, pleasurable and comfortable? The answer is not chores, academics, a task list or brushing their teeth. Also, as our world evolves, the idea that a person has to work hard to have a productive adult life becomes more and more intangible in the minds of children.

Separation anxiety is a real thing, but for most children that's not exactly what's occurring. A child may display anxiousness or fear not because they've developed a clinical disorder, but they have become overdependent on particular people and certain experiences. It is possible that there was a time of adjustment and your child was anxious due to the context of the situation. Now, though, after some time has passed, your child may still demonstrate symptoms of anxiety; but the driving force behind your child's responses may be a developed overdependence on the comfort of certain people and certain situations.

Such was the case for Alexi who melted down at times when his mother was not right there with him. Upon closer examination into Alexi's life, his caregivers and I discovered that when Alexi was otherwise entertained, he had no problem functioning well without his mom and was never "scared" without her during those times. When Alexi was not with people having fun or doing something he really enjoyed, he would express tremendous fear in the form of a meltdown if his mom wasn't present. In essence, mom had become Alexi's ever-present entertainment and servant.

With these scenarios we've been discussing and countless others, children become internally motivated to continue to express the symptoms of the various problems because the potential outcome is extremely desirable to them.

Hidden Rewards

Hidden rewards can motivate children to perpetuate maladaptive behaviors, even if they get into trouble. Although the behavior may be mind-boggling to adults, a child can find "good" reasons for troubling behavior. Hidden "rewards" for children include:

- A chance to possibly get what they want
- A chance to get out of what they don't want
- The excitement of the conflict
- The immediate gratification acting on impulses often brings
- Feeling powerful and in control of others
- Stealing the attention away from siblings and others
- Pulling others into their whirlpool of misery
- People feeling sorry for them instead of angry with them
- Influencing people to back off
- Responsibility lessened

Your child continues to have the problems he is having because the hidden rewards your child is experiencing is more powerful than the rewards you offer and the discipline implemented.

Internal Motivations, Temperament and Empowerment

More often than not, your child is internally motivated to continue the maladaptive behavior. Fred may have witnessed his dad display aggressiveness, yet Fred is his own person. Genetics and modeling cannot force a child to behave aggressively. Many caregivers are hurting from what they went through and what they see their child going through, therefore they put the responsibility on the adult instead of focusing on empowering the child.

Genetic predisposition is not genetic predetermination. Your child can live her own life free from aggressive, destructive behavior regardless of what she's experienced or who she's related to. Your child has a much greater chance of being driven towards aggressive behavior by acting in line with her own feelings and impulses and having this behavior

31

reinforced by one or more of the hidden rewards above than by what she witnessed in the past. The good news is that when we focus on the truth of your child's own struggle, we can empower her to develop the strength to overcome it.

Arthur is mentally neither unequipped nor under-equipped to focus or follow through with tasks. Arthur is under-motivated from within to consistently do so at certain times and in certain situations. Arthur has shown he can focus when well-motivated and when he gets to focus on something he values pouring his energy into. Arthur can focus. We've just got to help him develop the internal strength and motivation to pour his energy into focusing when he needs to instead of only when he wants to.

This is also true for Jasmine. Jasmine is not throwing tantrums driven by bullying or the teachers not doing their job at school. She is also not reacting to trauma. Jasmine is escaping sitting down and doing her work in the midst of the tantrum. The power of the immediate gratification of the tantrum outweighs the power of the consequences for Jasmine because the adults, in their confusion about what's wrong, do not focus responsibility for self-control on Jasmine. Even when her mom does, the discipline is watered down and inconsistent because her mom is not confident about holding her accountable for behavior that she is not sure her daughter can control.

A ubiquitous phenomena with our children is an internal natural fear of males that they do not have of females. This unspoken phenomena is why children typically behave better for male coaches, teachers, counselors, family members, friends, and even strangers. This caution around males does not apply for some children, but it does for most. This response is not indicative of a man being harsh or prone to anger, nor should it ever be.

An eight-year-old boy sat in my office. I inquired, "It seems from what your caregivers tell me that you listen to Dad more than Mom. Do you think that's true?" The boy shook his head up and down emphatically. I asked him, "Why do you think you listen to Dad more than Mom?" He replied, "Because Dad is scary." Countless children I've counseled have echoed the sentiments of this eight-year-old, even though most are like this boy's caregivers...dedicated, loving and non-abusive.

This hidden internal factor is more often why kids give female caregivers the most difficult time of all. It seems that "being there" should earn the respect of children when, unfortunately, it does not. Women, on average, have to work two to four times as hard as a man to earn the same respect from a child, especially a strong-willed child.

Your child doesn't lack the raw ability to stop himself from hitting, to be responsible, display respect, control himself when angry or be perfectly okay when away from you. Your child is just not in a place yet with the strength and motivation to consistently operate in line with these healthy choices. When we empower your child effectively to change his internal motivations, the outward results will be astounding.

Whether due to the power of your child's own temperament driving her and/or the power of what's comfortable, easy, or more rewarding to her, your child has continued to struggle from the inside out. The way to effectively help your child succeed is to help her build the skills and alter her will from the inside out. Trying to power a child to change through factors such as reward systems, discipline marred by misinformation, confusion and inconsistency, medication, and external changes in the child's life are temporary helps at best.

Your child's behavior is ill-fitting from the perspective of where we want our children to be; however, based on your child's internal motivations, subsequent experiences and where he is in his world, your child's behavior actually fits. When we understand the true internal motivations of a child, learn and remove hidden rewards, and operate effectively accordingly, we are on a path to empowering your child to transform. Transformation means your child develops the skills and will to maintain change from the inside out.

Next we look at the final major piece to the puzzle concerning what's likely driving your child's challenges: the environment. We'll allow God to give us wisdom about how reactions to environmental factors are often more powerful influences on our children than the environmental factors themselves.

CHAPTER 5

ENVIRONMENT

"It is our hypothesis that personality is shaped by the constant interplay of temperament and environment."
—New York Longitudinal Study

Significant changes in the environment of a child such as divorce, moving, death, loss, witnessing abuse and more can impact the way a child feels and behaves. Significant life changes often affect the stability and structure of a child's environment. We know that a family breakup, a traumatic event, a significant loss, a caregiver struggling with major health issues, substance abuse and/or financial issues affect a child; however, for most children 12 and under, the greatest impact of the event will be from the responses to the event, not the event itself.

Factually, a child can have significant emotional and behavior problems influenced by traumatic events and have significant emotional and behavior problems not influenced by traumatic events. We pay close attention when a child has been traumatized, yet we must also recognize a child can have the most significant emotional outbursts and behavior problems as well as traumatic events, and with surprising frequency, the two are not correlated.

For children with attitude and behavior problems, most of the time we are actually witnessing an interplay of powerful environmental factors to the child and temperament operating within the child. The problem is that both the significant environmental factors and inner temperament powerfully affecting most children are unknown, unconsidered or assessed incorrectly. The reason that children continue to get worse instead of better is that professionals and caregivers are reacting to help the child in light of how they assess that the outer factor may affect the child instead of recognizing that those very reactions are often the most powerful influence enabling the problems to perpetuate. Let's look at real-life examples to help us see the true energizing factors of the ongoing problems of many children. Kassidi, Jacob, Sam, Buckley and Jasmine will help us understand further.

Environment and Reactions

Kassidi's caregivers divorced when she was four years old. Kassidi's caregivers considered what was in her best interest and worked with that foundation throughout their split. Both of Kassidi's caregivers felt bad for Kassidi, especially her mom, even four years later. Eight-year-old Kassidi was brought to my office for major problems with focus, listening, defiance, tantrums, and aggression towards her caregivers.

Jacob was three years old when brought to me by his mother, Julie. Jacob was a bright, sweet terror. Jacob had significant problems with back talk, not listening, and throwing tantrums. Jacob had lived almost his entire young life with his mom and dad in his dad's parents' house. Julie and Freddie, Jacob's father, were working hard saving for their own place. When Freddie and Julie were at work, in-home care for Jacob was provided lovingly by Freddie's parents. Jacob's grandparents doted on their only grandson and treated him like a king.

Sam's dad, John, was involved in his life sporadically. His mom, Tina, was there for him every day. At 12 years old, Sam would do everything his dad told him whenever he came around but his mom, Tina, who cared for him daily, had to tell him something ten times before he would do it. Sam would also do what his football coaches told him, but didn't listen well to his female teachers.

Jasmine was a bright child who was brought to my office when she was five years old. Jasmine did not act out at home. Her mother was consistent with reinforcing healthy behavioral expectations. Jasmine did well in preschool behaviorally until kindergarten. This is literally when all h-e-double hockey sticks broke loose. Jasmine began throwing tantrums in school and within a month after kindergarten began, she was throwing chairs, hitting peers, falling down on the floor and disrupting the entire class four to five days per week.

Buckley was being raised by his grandmother. Buckley couldn't focus. He could "hyperfocus" for hours on video games, but couldn't focus in class or on his homework. Buckley's grandmother was told his brain made it difficult for him to tune out distractions except when he was able to "hyperfocus." Buckley had been on psychotropic medication for years, yet his problems with focusing and with irresponsibility continued to get worse.

Now let's look at each case a little more in-depth to discover the hidden interplays between these children, their environment and their internal temperament.

Both of Kassidi's caregivers felt bad for her post divorce, so they did what many caregivers do: the fun increased and the "getting on to" decreased. Both of Kassidi's caregivers backed off considerably in the structure they provided for her. Kassidi enjoyed being the boss, and her problems manifested primarily when her caregivers tried to "be the boss" and have her do something she didn't want to do. Kassidi knew her caregivers felt sorry for her and played this time and time again as her "get out of jail free" card.

Kassidi's parents thought their divorce four years prior was one of the primary factors driving their daughter's present problems. The fact that Kassidi's problems began and then escalated post divorce furthered the belief that the divorce was the culprit. For Kassidi, her parents divorcing was extremely hard on her. She still asked if they would ever get back together; however, her parents handled the divorce and the resulting co-parenting well. Reacting to the guilt of the divorce and feeling bad for Kassidi caused her parents to become extremely permissive with her, unintentionally empowering Kassidi to operate in line with the strong-willed temperament. When Kassidi's parents understood their daughter's inner battle to have life on her terms and empowered her to win this battle from the inside out, Kassidi got and stayed better.

Julie worked hard to provide structure and consistent discipline for Jacob, but she fought a daily battle with her in-laws. Jacob's grandparents couldn't bear to see him in trouble. Whenever Freddie, and primarily Julie, tried to correct Jacob for back talk, not listening, or throwing a tantrum, the grandparents would admonish them to "let Jacob be a kid!" Julie and Freddie were undermined constantly.

When Fred and Julie shifted focus away from the transitions of life affecting their son to how the interactions in the family were affecting him, the situation changed. Julie stood up to her in-laws respectfully and courageously to put a stop to all undermining. Fred backed her up. Julie then focused on believing in herself and her son, empowering them both to focus on Jacob consistently displaying respectful behavior to adults.

Sam's mom thought Sam loved his dad more than he loved her. She was frustrated that she was there for him daily, yet he treated her with such disrespect and his dad with such respect. She also thought maybe Sam's dad was to blame for Sam's disrespectful behavior towards women because he acted disrespectfully towards women.

Sam was like countless kids who do not have an internal natural fear of his mom and females, therefore he gave them a hard time. Even though his dad was not there much, Sam's natural fear of his dad caused him to show him respect almost without fail. As we've previously discussed, children typically have a natural fear of males that they do not have of females. This is a naturally occurring ubiquitous phenomena. Understanding this helped Sam's mom accept that she wasn't a failure, take the focus off blaming Sam's dad and place the focus on empowering Sam to respect her. She did have to work hard to help Sam develop respect for her and other women, but when she put together her cohesive Plan, she was able to help Sam transform. This alleviated her fears that Sam was doomed to turn out as a womanizer.

Jasmine's mom was consistent and lovingly firm in their home life. When Jasmine began having meltdowns in school out of nowhere, this was extremely confusing to everyone. Jasmine's mom disciplined her at home for her behavior in school, but didn't do so consistently because she didn't know what caused Jasmine to have these problems. Was it the teachers, the environment, bullying? Had something happened to Jasmine? Was Jasmine bored because she was so smart, seeking attention, or did she have a disorder she couldn't control? All of this left Jasmine's mom feeling disempowered, confused, frustrated and scared for Jasmine's future.

There was no strong evidence to link the root of the tantrums to any specific environmental factor. Discussing the motivations of a child operating with the strong-willed temperament and understanding the hidden rewards that Jasmine was likely experiencing for tantrums shed new light on what was wrong with Jasmine. This allowed Jasmine's mom and me to discuss what to do about it, specifically aimed at empowering Jasmine to redirect her energy away from tantrums and into self-discipline, to do what she ought to do regardless of her feelings. You see, like many children, Jasmine's struggle with self-discipline, with not wanting to push herself to focus and do her schoolwork, led to the struggle with self-control, i.e. tantrums.

Buckley had trouble with focusing in school, homework, chores and other responsibilities. Professionals diagnosed Buckley with ADHD. His grandmother was told this meant he had problems in his brain chemistry that limited his ability to focus and display responsible behavior. When Mildred was confused by how Buckley could focus for hours on YouTube videos or his games, she was told that people with ADHD have a phenomena called "hyperfocusing." Mildred was getting overwhelmed and worn down with Buckley not doing his homework, not paying attention in school and having to tell him over and over every day to do the same tasks.

Mildred was confused about how to help Buckley. She wanted him to be more responsible, yet didn't know what he was capable of. She didn't want to be mean to him if he truly couldn't focus, so she had no confidence in holding his feet to the fire in any area of responsibility. It wasn't that Buckley couldn't focus, do his homework or be responsible with his chores, although this seemed to be the case. When Buckley was offered a big reward or had an upcoming activity in which he really wanted to participate, he demonstrated an ability to focus and follow through with tasks, even several at a time, because he was motivated to do so.

Mildred acknowledged that Buckley could focus well on what he enjoyed and even what he didn't enjoy when motivated. We used this information to believe in Buckley's raw ability to focus and follow through with tasks. We empowered him until he developed the self-discipline necessary to focus and follow through consistently. Buckley gained powerful skills in the area of focus and responsibility as well as self-confidence.

Environment and Temperamental Affinity

The New York Longitudinal Study gave us the idea of innate temperament from this statement: "...personality is shaped by the constant interplay of temperament and environment." Due to temperament being malleable, I call it "temperamental affinity."

Children operate with a dominant temperamental affinity. This affinity is how your child is motivated internally. Does your child seem primarily motivated to: A) Please and Achieve; B) Avoid the Spotlight; or C) Get her Way? You may see characteristics of more than one or all of these; however, connected to the main concerns you have for your child, which seems to be driving your child most often?

The vast majority of children displaying the most significant emotional and/or behavior problems are operating with the strong-willed temperamental affinity. Children operating with the strong-willed temperamental affinity are driven from within to get their way, to have life on their terms. If this is the case for your child, guilt, overcompensating, disbelief in your child's capabilities, inconsistencies caused by confusion, overprotectiveness, quarreling with other caregivers and being undermined are quite possibly the most powerful factors influencing your child today rather than the trials, trauma, and transitions of the past.

Developing Brain, Temperament and Environment Roundup

We are often led to look for reasons for our children's problems in the wrong places, which has the appearance of wisdom but is often simply a deception fueled by the enemy to undermine our children's potential. Your child's brain is likely not dysfunctional. Your child is likely not disordered, at least not where the core issues related to the emotional and behavior problems are concerned. Your child is likely not incapable, despite how he might appear. You are not a failure, despite how you might feel.

I hope what you've read to this point has helped you understand some identifiable truths. Your child's brain is developing. Your child, and thus many of your child's problems, are likely driven at this point from within, often in line with the strong-willed temperamental affinity. It is quite possible, even likely, that your child's current problems may be more influenced by reactions in the environment in conjunction with his temperamental affinity than with events themselves.

John 8:32 tells us, *"Then you will know the truth, and the truth will set you free."* God wants you to be free to empower your child through faith to reach his or her potential. He wants you all to be free of the confusion and misery. This freedom comes when we seek and embrace the truth about what's wrong with your child. Your child is capable. Your child needs you in order to succeed. You are capable. Your child will succeed with your help.

Now we devise a specifically tailored Plan to effectively empower your child to transform. Embrace the truth that when we do this correctly and thoroughly, your Plan will work. Now that we've uncovered the truths that answer the first question—"What's wrong with my child?"—let's answer the second most important caregiver question together: "What do I do about it?"

In faith, we L.E.A.P.

CHAPTER 6

WHAT DO I DO ABOUT IT? L.E.A.P.

What L.E.A.P. Is

L.E.A.P. stands for Love, Expectation of Excellence, Affirming Accountability and Perseverance. I love acronyms and concise ways of categorizing information. Hopefully this acrostic helps you easily remember the key foundational elements to revolutionize your process to end the problems.

L.E.A.P. is effective, essential, and empowering to you and your child. L.E.A.P. is not a gimmick. L.E.A.P. is proven in the results of the countless people who are implementing these principles with amazing success. L.E.A.P. comprises the essential elements you need to put your purposeful Plan together. L.E.A.P. is a guide to success in helping your child overcome any and every problem within his ability to do so, which entails most of them. The L.E.A.P. process is most effectively implemented with children between the ages of four and twelve. It is imperative that children evidence the mental and emotional maturity to comprehend and put into practice the strategies in order for the L.E.A.P. process to be successful.

L.E.A.P. is:

Love
Expectation of Excellence
Affirming Accountability
Perseverance

Love is about relationship, chasing the heart of your child.

Expectation of Excellence is a challenge to excellence, not perfection.

Af irming accountability actionizes "I believe in you; therefore, I hold you to an Expectation of Excellence."

Perseverance is bringing consistency and conviction to bear until your child builds the skills to overcome the problem.

What L.E.A.P. AIN'T

L.E.A.P. ain't a quick-fix, stand alone "miracle pill" to your belabored problems. L.E.A.P. is a guide that comprises essential elements you need for success for you and your child. Not only is it empowering when we put our faith in God's design and L.E.A.P., but we have to do this together. If there were easy fixes to your child's problems, you would have done them already. Though they might not be easy, you will be able to develop answers with my help. You are the expert on your child; I am the expert in the field. Together, we will help your child overcome his problems.

L.E.A.P. ain't without power. L.E.A.P. ain't without providence. L.E.A.P. ain't without proof. L.E.A.P. ain't going to fail you, so don't you fail. Don't fail to do the work, to put your Plan together with this guide. You have and always have had the ability to help your child transform. Take a L.E.A.P. of faith in this process by pouring your energy into it. See it through. God ain't going to fail you. You ain't going to fail.

Build, Not Just Behave

From this point forward, it's all about helping your child transform. You understand now that your child is designed by God to succeed with your help. Your conviction and consistency will help your child build, not just behave. The exciting thing is that your child will build character, confidence and essential life skills as the foundation for overcoming the problems. This will allow your child to get stronger from the inside out.

Plan to take a L.E.A.P. of faith with God, yourself and your child. Develop your Plan first. When you're done, and not before, implement your Plan to L.E.A.P. with consistency and conviction. Your process will create powerful opportunities for your child to conquer her specific problems, now and forever.

What Is This "Plan" You Keep Referring to, AJ?

You are going to enter a training process with your child, and battles will ensue. Before soldiers go into battle, they strategize. Get prepared for the battle of wills and wits that is about to ensue in earnest. Your training will help you prepare to break your child's will while in no way crushing your child's spirit. You must accomplish both. The L.E.A.P. elements will guide you as we construct your Plan, together.

Your work with the L.E.A.P. process and adding other essential elements you need will move you from the 70% to 80% range of the Most Effective Actions on a daily basis to help your child succeed (that you are already doing) into the 97% to 98% range. Planning and strategizing how to be 97% to 98% effective on a daily basis to help your child succeed will take time, but it will be time well spent. Although it will take more time on the front end to develop a solid, effective Plan to help your child conquer his problems, the more solid your Plan, the more effective it will be to accomplish your goals efficiently.

Imagine that you have a bucket. With it, you will help build an aquarium, but your bucket has a few holes in it. In order to accomplish your goal, the aquarium has to be filled with water. Would it be more beneficial for you to spend time up front repairing your bucket or trying to accomplish your goal with frustrating holes that undermine your effectiveness?

When I was a kid, I loved a series of books called "Choose Your Own Adventure." The cool thing about these books was that you didn't read the whole book. You made choices along the way that would lead you down different paths to different sections of the books. If you wanted, you could make different choices for different story experiences. I was fascinated by these books. Around the age of eight, I walked out of the library one day with a stack of them I could barely carry. A woman exclaimed, "Wow, what a reader!" If she only knew.

This is your story, your Plan. I am the expert in the field; you are the expert on your child. Only you know exactly what you need for your child. I've had some caregivers that just needed to know that the problem their child was having was likely within her ability to control and overcome with help. Once these caregivers knew the truth, they took off with their own Plan unencumbered. Most caregivers want and/or need to develop a detailed Plan in order to have a sound and effective process. Some want to read everything and then decide for themselves. Just like the choose-your-own-adventure books, there is no singular right or wrong way; your Plan must choose the way that is right for you and your child.

Find the path inside yourself using the following guide. Embrace that God gave you the child in your care for a reason. He chose you and has given you everything you need to succeed. As your guide in the process, my goal is to give you tested information to use to develop **your** most effective Plan. You will craft your Plan tailored to the needs of your child, and you will be successful.

The information I share in the rest of the book has come from three sources:

1. The wisdom God has shared with me

2. Testing these theories with the children God gave me to raise
3. Working with thousands of kids and families and seeing what has consistently worked and not worked for them

What we will discuss has been proven by real people to be effective. God has led me to share insights gathered by spending thousands of hours meeting with thousands of people just like you. My confidence comes from the effectiveness people find by consistently employing these strategies.

Choose what you need to develop your most effective Plan to help your child succeed. I caution you, though, not to move forward with any noticeable or significant changes with your child until your Plan is solidified. Starting something unprepared that falls apart will likely cause your child to sink deeper into her problems and believe she just has to fight you harder to maintain the status quo. You don't want that. Develop your Plan fully. Identify the 70% to 80% of the Most Effective Actions you are already doing, then tweak what you are doing to reach that 97% to 98% effectiveness. Move forward with courage, conviction and consistency. Remember, courage comes before confidence.

Steps to Transformation

1. Understand each element of L.E.A.P. and prepare to live them.
2. Use the Resource Guide to consolidate your Plan.
3. Communicate your Expectation of Excellence with a brief discussion.
4. Implement your Plan.
5. Persevere.

I have faith in God, you and your child. We do not fail as caregivers when we love our children the best we can. We aren't here to control them or make them be what we want them to be. We are here to guide them the best we can. You will choose your own adventure in guiding your child.

Remember, regardless of what we do, our children get to choose their own adventure. Without compromise, let's just make the loving, beneficial path hard to resist. Let's take this L.E.A.P. together.

A Few Can L.E.A.P Rather Quickly

Jamie was a single mom who moved back into her mom's house when she fell on hard times. Jamie had a wonderful eight-year-old daughter, Mariah, who was beautiful in the Lord, rambunctious and free. Unfortunately, these characteristics did not work well at school. Jamie came into my office exasperated with Mariah's behavior....and Jamie had a major attitude! She wanted me to "fix" Mariah. As we talked over several sessions, I communicated that I couldn't fix Mariah because the power lay with Jamie and Mariah. I shared that I wanted to empower Jamie to empower Mariah.

Ultimately, Jamie revealed the truth as she shared, "I was a consistent, firm, loving and dedicated mom. When I moved in with my own mom, I gave in to her pressure and undermining. My daughter never used to act like this, but now I back down and give Mariah her way; and it's ruining her. Also, I started trying to do all these new strategies, like rewarding, that I know don't work for my daughter; but it was easier than battling my mom."

Jamie, in that moment, became resolved to do once again what her child needed her to do. I saw the look of determination and a big chunk of her confidence return immediately. Jamie took her power back. Jamie didn't need to go through the steps as many do. Jamie needed to get back on track with what she knew was right for her daughter and what she knew worked.

I didn't share Jamie's story to communicate to you that there is a quick fix for your child's problems. I am sharing this story for the relatively small percentage of you out there who got away from a strong foundation and need to get back to it. But about 90% or more of caregivers find their effectiveness through being thorough with the L.E.A.P. process.

CHAPTER 7

LOVE – THE FIRST STEP OF L.E.A.P.

"We love Him, because He first loved us."

—1 John 4:19

I have heard it said, "Love is not what God does; love is who He is." He is who He says He is and is everything He wants us to be. 1 John 4:7, and continuing through the end of the chapter, shares God's love for us. Check it out. It might take only a minute to see how much God loves you. Rules will take us only so far. Rules without relationship will cause destruction. In order to build on a firm foundation, our children must know that we love them.

The heart of the truth is that to empower your child to push her energy away from non-beneficial choices and toward beneficial choices, your child needs firm, effective, consistent discipline. Your child, 12 and under, is a choice-and-consequence learner developmentally. To empower your child to push her energy into healthy decisions, you must effectively connect choice to consequence.

We caregivers must confront our own fears and discomfort with the idea of firm discipline and remove these barriers from empowering our kids according to their needs. We must gain wisdom, understanding and truth, empowering us to love our child as God does:

*And have you forgotten the encouraging words God spoke to
you as his children? He said, "My child, don't make light of
the Lord's discipline, and don't give up when he corrects you.
For the Lord disciplines those he loves, and he punishes each
one he accepts as his child."*

—Hebrews 12: 5-6, NLT

Love and discipline are always one in the same to God. We must find
a way to make it so with us. For the benefit of your child, when necessary,
your child will need your lovingly firm and effective discipline. God loves
us no matter what we do whether He approves of our choice or not. Our
action message to our children is, " I love you and accept you always, but
I may or may not, depending on what is healthy and beneficial for you,
approve of and accept the choice that you make. I will not punish you due
to the hurt your choice causes me, but when necessary to encourage you
away from destructive choices in your life."

Some people will always twist the truth of lovingly firm discipline
into an excuse to take out their anger, sorrow and pain on a child. This is
not who we are. Yes, we as caregivers make mistakes. All of us caregivers
likely have made or will make a mistake verbally or physically that unfairly
hurts our child—but such mistakes should be extremely rare. When this
occurs, love requires us to own our mistake, repent, forgive ourselves, seek
forgiveness and commit to change.

Love also requires us to seek wisdom and discernment between lovingly firm discipline (including firm and appropriate spankings) and abuse.
Lovingly firm discipline from a caregiver is mostly selfless. It effectively connects unhealthy choice to the consequence of a measured amount of pain.
Built on the foundation of a loving relationship, this empowers your child to
put less energy into unhealthy choices and more energy into beneficial ones.
Abuse is selfish. Abuse uses excuses to pour out pain on the child in measures
unfair and inequitable to the situation.

The enemy wants to blur the lines between lovingly firm discipline
and abuse to cripple our children by crippling our empowerment of them.

We must use God-given wisdom to apply lovingly firm discipline in the measure most beneficial based on the needs of our child while avoiding abuse. We must also rally to promote the truth that lovingly firm discipline on the foundation of a loving relationship, as we'll discuss in this section of the book, is extremely healthy and beneficial to children 12 and under.

Feelings...Nothing More Than Feelings

We caregivers must also build the empowerment of our child's transformation on the basis of another immutable truth: Our Feelings Don't Matter. Wow...there...I wrote it! Before you grab the torch for the book burning, allow me to explain.

First, the most important question in whether you or another caregiver can be a key figure in disciplining your child is this: Does your child know that the caregiver disciplining him loves him?

Notice the question is not, "Does the caregiver disciplining your child love your child?" This is not enough. Your child must know in his own heart that the caregiver implementing lovingly firm discipline loves him.

Without a child being certain in her own heart that a caregiver enacting firm discipline loves her, confusion can creep in about the caregiver's motives. If a child doubts the caregiver's motives, resentment that can undermine everything often forms. You may have heard, "Discipline without relationship creates rebellion." I assure you that discipline without relationship creates resentment...and resentment creates rebellion.

Any caregiver who your child is not convinced loves him must not enact lovingly firm discipline. Some caregivers are trying to enact firm discipline without a strong relational foundation with their child. Some caregivers are allowing other caregivers that your child does not absolutely know loves him to enact firm discipline. If either of these scenarios are the case, this must be changed immediately to avoid pernicious resentment from undermining your efforts and relationship. Allow the relationship to build with boundaries and communication, but the caregiver must hold off on taking a primary role in enacting firm discipline until the relational bond is strong. When the child has no doubt, in truth, that she is loved by the caregiver, lovingly firm discipline can commence.

In addition, regardless of how you may feel, any caregiver your child knows loves him can enact lovingly firm discipline. Some of you have protected your child from such caregivers when your child knows the person loves him, even if he complains about the caregiver "being mean." No one wants their child to be mistreated or abused; however, due to their own feelings and experiences, many caregivers are protecting their children from other caregivers who could be lovingly firm and effective through appropriate discipline with their child.

Pray for wisdom and seek objective and/or professional advice. Discern beyond feelings, personal experiences and hurt-driven verbalizations the truth of your child's heart and needs. Just like the pain of an appropriate spanking doesn't leave any bruises on the body, discipline in the context of a loving relationship doesn't leave any bruises on the heart. Any pain of lovingly firm discipline on the body and heart, built on the foundation of the loving relationship, will only be transient. This is where you'll see signs of your child still wanting to be close to you even though you inflicted the pain of firm and appropriate discipline. Sometimes it will be surprising how quickly after you've disciplined your child that they will come and cuddle up next to you. When discipline and relationship are done right, your child will have no doubt in her mind that you mean business and no doubt in her heart that you love her.

Sam

Sam was incredulous at the idea that he and Jackie stop focusing on disciplining Jackie's ten-year-old daughter, Janet, whose behavior was out of control. Janet was a handful to Jackie as a single mom. When Sam came along, Jackie was thankful to have a friend she trusted. She was hesitant to allow Sam to step in and help with discipline, but Sam proved that he genuinely cared about Janet early in their relationship.

Jackie worked long hours, and the lack of time with Janet weakened their relational bond significantly. Sam's career was more flexible and he could work from home, allowing him to be there with Janet more. Both, though, at the time, did not have a strong relational foundation with Janet in which to build lovingly firm discipline. Trusting in the truth of prioritizing relationship over discipline, Sam and Jackie sought wisdom and made changes.

First, Sam and Jackie agreed that Jackie would be the primary disciplinarian. Jackie had been Janet's caregiver her whole life, giving her a leg up in Janet understanding that her mom cared for her. Sam would set boundaries and communicate effectively anything in his relationship with Janet that was not acceptable, but only Jackie held Janet accountable through discipline when needed. It wasn't that Sam had no power; it was that Jackie empowered Janet to be respectful of Sam based on her Expectation of Excellence.

Jackie focused specifically on empowering Janet to be respectful while making changes in her life and career to spend an adequate amount of intentional time with Janet. Janet had many behavior problems at home and school, but Sam and Jackie focused on strengthening their relationship with Janet until she understood without a doubt that both her mom and stepfather Sam loved her. Confusion was cleared for Janet because she knew her mom cared about *her* and not only about her behaving so she wouldn't interfere with her mom's career. Also, after being hurt by someone else who had previously left Janet and her mother heartbroken, Janet finally reached the point where she trusted Sam's commitment to the both of them.

When the relational bonds strengthened, Sam and Jackie intensified their efforts to empower Janet to change her behavior through Affirming Accountability. Building all accountability with lovingly firm discipline on the strength of the loving relationship allowed Janet to accept that discipline was only about their desire to see her make better choices. Ultimately, Janet stopped pouring her energy into fighting for power and started pouring it instead into disciplining herself to be respectful regardless of how she felt.

Sarah

Sarah had been physically abused by her ex-husband Tom, Billy's father, during their marriage. Sarah did not trust Tom. The court provided Tom joint visitation during their divorce proceedings. Sarah was often heartbroken when Billy would tell her after a visit with his dad that Tom had been mean to him, even though there were no verifiable signs of abuse.

Sarah displayed a courage, faith and conviction that few women do. Sarah sought help for her own pain and conquered her fear of and prejudices against Tom. She sought support and help to be as objective as possible when it came to Tom and Billy's relationship. She eventually understood that Tom did love Billy and the "meanness" Billy complained about was when Tom tried to effectively discipline his son appropriately. Sarah also recognized that her own hurts caused her to immediately side with her son when he would complain about his father.

Tom still struggled with treating Sarah well at times. Sarah made sure she had firm boundaries between her and Tom so she couldn't be manipulated or mistreated. She empowered herself to overcome her past in a way that allowed her son to be empowered in the present. Sarah, understanding that her son knew that his dad loved him, courageously began to trust her son to his dad even though she didn't personally trust Tom. She monitored the situation closely and began to support Tom's disciplining of Billy when he needed it. Sarah's courage allowed her to act in truth and love, which empowered Billy's transformation.

Renault

Renault did not think his son's mom was a good mom. Renault never had problems with their son like Gina had. Renault was willing to admit he had a supercilious attitude towards Gina and was not helpful at best and disparaging towards her caregiving at worst. Renault showed gravitas in pushing aside his pride to accept the fact that, in most households, children treat men very differently than they treat women.

Renault allowed himself to understand that most children have a natural fear of men that they do not have of women. Yes, Renault meant business and set an expectation of respect between him and his son; however, he discounted Gina's uphill battle. Renault decided to acknowledge the truth that his son knew his mom loved him. He challenged himself to be completely respectful of Gina and supportive of his son's internal development of respect. Renault's change in attitude empowered his son to push his energy into being respectful to his mom and other women in authority instead of pushing to "be the boss."

Second Most Important Reason Our Feelings Don't Matter

Some of you don't feel much love for your child right now. Some of you feel guilty because you honestly don't want to be around your child right now. Many caregivers wrestle with feelings such as these at different stages. The second most important reason why these feelings don't matter is, love is not a feeling. According to 1 Corinthians 13: 4-7:

- Love is patient.
- Love is kind.
- Love is not envious.
- Love is not boastful.
- Love is not proud.
- Love is not dishonoring of others.

- Love is not self-seeking.
- Love is not easily angered.
- Love keeps no record of wrongs.
- Love does not delight in evil.
- Love rejoices with the truth.
- Love always protects
- Love always trusts.
- Love always hopes.
- Love always perseveres.

God's love is displayed through us in what we do. Love is independent of our feelings and often happens regardless of our feelings. Ever tried to be patient with your child when you didn't feel like it? Ever chose to help your child when you didn't really want to? Ever stuck with discipline you knew was best for your child when you wanted to give in? Ever cared for your child to the best of your ability despite your feelings?

Regardless of how you feel, regardless of any mistakes, you are primarily acting with love on a daily basis towards your child. You are human if you don't feel love right now for your child—not a monster. Continue to increase your loving actions. Choose to be patient with yourself. Try to be a little slower to get angry. Embrace hope. When we practice any aspect of Godly love, we demonstrate love to the other person, to God and to ourselves, all at the same time, every time.

Rose

Maybe you dreamed about having the child that's in your care, maybe you didn't. Regardless, you likely never thought raising a child could be as tough as it is. Rose and her husband dreamed about adopting. When they finally were able to bring Ben home, they knew this was a fulfillment of their God-given hope. Rose, however, never dreamed she would have the intense hurt, anger and depression that came with raising a troubled child.

Rose wrestled with emotional pain because she believed God wanted her and her husband to adopt six-year-old Ben; but she did not feel love for him. Ben's attitude and behavior were terrible and Rose, as his primary caregiver, had to deal with the brunt of Ben's troubles. Rose felt incredible guilt because she couldn't understand why she felt so awful towards Ben if she was raising the child that God wanted her and her husband to raise.

Rose chose to face and accept her own feelings. She accepted God's grace and stopped beating herself up for the way she felt. Rose recognized she was treating Ben with love every day through her actions regardless of how she felt. She made tweaks in her actions to convey her love purely, such as significantly reducing her yelling at Ben. Rose also made a personal commitment to spend intentional time with Ben daily, even if he was in trouble. Rose poured energy into the principles in this book, persevering until Ben transformed. It was a long, difficult road for Rose, but she grew tremendously through the journey.

You may or may not feel like you love or even like the child that has compelled you to read this book. That is normal. Unconditional love is not "like." You can feel that you don't like your child or even love your child because love is not a feeling. When we feel angry with our children, we will have angry thoughts that are normal. In these thoughts, countless loving caregivers have thought about slapping, hitting, punching, choking, leaving, slamming their children against the wall or countless other wrongs. I have had some of these thoughts cross my mind as a caregiver in the midst of pain in raising my children.

These thoughts crossing our minds, in and of themselves, is not bad or a sign of unhealthy emotions; however, there is a firm line...do not dwell on these thoughts and never act on these impulses. Acting on these thoughts is not love. *"Be ye angry and sin not"* (Ephesians 4:26, KJV). We can be filled with the feeling of anger and act with love each time. For the sake of our children, we must discern our feelings and thoughts from our actions and choose to act only to build up our children, according to their needs, not our own.

We caregivers can choose to see beyond our hurt, our confusion, and the feelings the enemy wants to use against us to steal, kill and destroy our efforts to empower our children effectively. We can courageously choose to keep chasing the heart of our child, regardless of how we feel or what they do. This can be difficult when our hearts are hurt and broken, like Rose's heart was. God is the only one who can heal our hearts and give us the courage and fortitude to keep acting in loving ways despite the hurt someone else is causing. I cannot tell you this is easy. It is not. I can remind us all though, that God has decreed that we and our children are worth it.

Stopping the Hurt

Sometimes the first step is stopping the hurt. Some relationships between caregivers and children have broken down to the point that it has led to a negative cycle of interaction. Caregivers may be frustrated, angry, and hurt; they may even feel like giving up with their children. These feelings are exacerbated when caregivers have tried so many different options to help their child without lasting results.

If the direction you are driving does not lead where you want to go, stop. Sometimes we are not even sure how to head in the right direction because we've been heading down a particular path so long. Stopping the hurt, the yelling, and the compromise takes courage—especially because many of you don't know what else to do. Try. Ask God for forgiveness, accept it, and push your energy away from guilt and bitterness and into acting with love for yourself and your child. Michael Jackson sang, "I'm starting with the man in the mirror." Look into the mirror of your relationship with your child. What can you do today to stop the cycle of hurt?

Sabrina & Rick

Sabrina brought her 11-year-old son Rick, whom she was raising by herself with the help of some of her family members, to see me. Rick was a bright young man, but his grades were suffering because he was not doing his work. Rick also was getting into a lot of trouble in school. He constantly had to be told to do chores at home and reminded about certain tasks and responsibilities almost every day. Rick would listen to his uncles and be motivated to improve for brief periods when they would talk to him or discipline him, but his mom seemed to get nowhere.

Sabrina was willing to look at herself. She assessed what she did that made Rick feel both loved and unloved, and also what she did that influenced Rick to trust and respect her or not. Sabrina screamed, yelled, and talked negatively to Rick not only out of frustration but because she thought he might be motivated by these actions to change. Rick did hate the screaming and discouraging comments, but they did not motivate him to change in any positive way.

Sabrina honestly examined many aspects of her life as a woman and a mother that impacted her relationship and her example to Rick. She decided to stop the hurt, even though she still felt hurt by her son's actions. She also confronted her own recreational marijuana use and repeated cycle of broken relationships with men. Sabrina stopped screaming, yelling, and putting Rick down because of his underachievement and lack of responsibility. Sabrina decided not to take her son's actions personally, but understood he was struggling to do the right thing. Sabrina focused on building her relationship with Rick. Sabrina chose to put her energy into life choices that influenced her son to trust and respect her decision-making. Her efforts in working on herself, along with addressing Rick's behavior with a solid Plan according to the principles in this book, ultimately encouraged Rick to cooperate with his mom.

What's Your Love Story?

We've discussed real-life love stories…love stories mixed with pain, yet ending in hope. We will continue your love story until your hopes for your child are fulfilled. Maybe you can confidently answer in the affirmative to the question, "Does your child know that the caregiver disciplining her loves her?" Maybe some tweaks need to be made. It may be beneficial for you to take a step back and seek wisdom. Whatever the case may be, we choose to love our children in the ways they need, not in ways that are convenient for us.

As we move forward to help you create your Plan to effectively empower your child to change on the foundation of a loving relationship, let's hold tight to the following truths:

- When your child knows he is loved, he can accept firm discipline.
- Discipline must always be molded by what love truly is.
- Discipline, done in love, shapes character in healthy ways.
- The loving relationship can contain every ounce of healthy discipline necessary to help your child succeed.

Embrace love. Our feelings don't matter because love is not based on feelings. Even Jesus asked his Father to spare Him from the cross if there was another way. He did not feel like being tortured, mocked, ridiculed, beaten, spat on and crucified. However, His feelings did not rule His actions; His love for us did.

Love yourself. Forgive yourself. Give yourself grace. Take a break when you need it. Say positive and hopeful words to yourself, then love your child. I'm not talking about your feelings, which may take some time to heal; I'm talking about your actions. Your hurt is not forever. Resolve that the hurting stops today.

Today, say words that challenge your child to change based on your belief in her. Today, speak calmly, firmly, concisely. Today, spend a little uninterrupted time with your child. Today, choose to examine what type and to what degree of lovingly firm discipline your child needs. Today, take note of your insights as you develop your solid Plan that will empower your child to transform. Today...live love.

You now have the foundation of the loving relationship, or are building it. Now we take the next step in developing your Plan to empower your child to build transforming skills from the inside out. Love compels us to raise the bar for your child and empower your child to grow in confidence and character by achieving new personal success. We now will help you identify and develop your Expectation of Excellence—the E in L.E.A.P.

CHAPTER 8

EXPECTATION OF EXCELLENCE

Believe in Your Child's Ability

> *"Where there is no vision, the people perish."*
> —Proverbs 29:18a, KJV

Expect excellence. Your child is capable of it. You may wonder, you may doubt this, you may be unsure, but your child can achieve the positive expectation you set with God's help and your empowerment along with other resources.

Expectation is synonymous with your goals, vision and hopes for your child. You are already on a path of healthy relationship with your child. A healthy relationship must always be where we begin. Now, envision the end of the journey. How will your child respond differently to her world at that time? Be specific in your mind's eye.

Your Expectation of Excellence will solidify what specifically you are leading your child toward. Your Plan will comprise your best route to travel. You will fight and help your child win only one major battle at a time. This creates the foundation to build success in both yourself and your child. Defining your expectation for your child is your next specific step in moving from doing 70% to 80% of the Most Effective Actions on a daily basis to help your child succeed to the 97% to 98% range.

Define Your Expectation

Defining your Expectation of Excellence for your child will be a three-step process:

1. Identify the main concern.
2. Specify your Expectation of Excellence.
3. Recognize the life skills.

Step 1: Identify the Main Concern

Think of the problems your child is having. Which specific problem do you feel you need to help your child overcome first?

Here are some examples from other caregivers:

- Hitting
- Not doing what she is told
- Tantrums
- Not following through with tasks
- Repeating incessantly
- Not focusing in the mornings
- Bedtime battles
- Running away when being disciplined
- Arguing/talking back
- Making excuses
- Screaming and yelling
- Shutting down
- Emotional outbursts

If it helps, feel free to jot down your short list of main concerns. All of your concerns are important. I want you to pick the one concern you believe is most foundational to help your child overcome first. The foundational concern may not be the one causing the most problems. The foundational main concern you help your child build the skills to overcome first must be one that sets up both of you for future success with other concerns.

Our focus is helping your child build change from the inside out. Concomitantly, empowerment must be solidified inside your relationship with your child and inside your home first and then extrapolated to other relationships and outside areas. For example, a child may have trouble respecting adults at school, yet also have trouble respecting adults at home. When caregivers focus on trying to empower their child to respect authority at school, their efforts are sabotaged by disrespect towards them at home. A caregiver may try to hold his child's feet to the fire about hitting peers at daycare, but that can be difficult when the child gets angry during discipline and attacks the caregiver.

You can't take anyone further than you've gone yourself. You are fighting a losing battle trying to take your child to a level of improvement you and your child don't yet have established between the two of you. Let's take a cue from airline safety protocols: "In the event of a loss of cabin pressure, place the oxygen mask on yourself before placing it on your child." Let's ensure you and your child are breathing the air of respect or responsibility consistently between you, then we will use this as a foundation on which to help your child remove the obstacles suffocating his potential in other areas of his life and relationships.

Grant

Grant's caregivers listed their main concerns as:

- Hitting his mom
- Talking back
- Impulsiveness
- Not listening to his parents
- Not following through with tasks

- Lack of focus and follow through in the morning
- Battling to get him to go to bed

When Grant's biological dad and mom, who co-parented apart, discussed these concerns, they narrowed it down to Grant not listening to them as their main concern to start with. Even though Grant hit and had other problems which were of tremendous concern, his mom and dad agreed that if Grant did what they told him, when they told him, this would resolve a lot of the other problems.

Grant's parents became aware of a pattern with their son that is common with many kids. The struggle with self-discipline, i.e. doing what they ought to do, most often led to Grant struggling with self-control, or controlling himself regardless of how he feels. When Grant's parents confronted him about not doing what he was told, he would often erupt into tantrums, running away or hitting. Grant's parents decided that even though the tantrums, running and hitting were worse problems, that when Grant did what he was told the first time, the situation would not escalate into screaming, throwing fits, and aggression. The foundational concern that Grant's parents decided to start with was Grant not listening to them.

Simon

Caregivers face many pressures when their child's struggle occurs in or is related to school. Pressures include but are not limited to their child failing, being labeled, being kicked out of school, feeling alienated or the caregivers getting in trouble with the law themselves. Simon's caregivers had major concerns for him concerning school.

Ten-year-old Simon had trouble listening, focusing, and following through with tasks at school and at home. His parents were more concerned about these problems affecting Simon with school, but decided that it would be best to start by helping Simon do well with listening, focusing and following through with tasks with them and at home first. The main concern that Simon's parents decided to address was the morning routine or lack thereof.

Simon's mom and dad fought with Simon almost every morning to get to school on time. Simon would not get out of bed. When he did get out of bed, he would not follow through with tasks. He'd stand in the bathroom staring in the mirror like he was in a daze or his parents would find him doing something else other than getting ready. They had to constantly be on Simon to do every little thing in the morning. For Simon's parents, every morning was the stuff of nightmares.

Simon's parents felt that a better morning was foundational for success in the family starting their day on a positive note. They accepted that their process would be stronger when they helped Simon listen, focus and follow through with tasks starting at home. Simon's parents courageously accepted that, in order to build a lasting process, Simon might fail in school in the short term. The idea of their son failing was extremely hard for Simon's parents. They decided to have faith in doing what was right for Simon long term instead of giving in to short-term pressures. They accepted that helping Simon improve listening, focusing and following through with tasks in the morning at home was the foundation on which to build his success at school.

Jasmine

If your child's problem that concerns you most isn't about your relationship or within your home, then you can focus on empowering her to transform in the other area of her life. Such was the case with Jasmine. Jasmine's mom basically had one main concern: throwing tantrums in school on almost a daily basis

Jasmine never threw tantrums at home because she had a healthy fear of her mom that she didn't have for most school staff. During Jasmine's tantrums at school, she would throw objects around the room, hit other kids, and be defiant towards teachers. As a single mom, it was hard to work while getting calls from school every day. Jasmine's mom decided to believe that her daughter was likely capable of controlling herself. She created a solid Plan built on their loving relationship, starting with her Expectation of Excellence for her daughter.

Your Foundational Main Concern

Once your child overcomes your specific main concern, you then will move to the next concern. You will help your child build a legacy of success overcoming one specific major concern at a time. Ask yourself these questions: Which specific main concern for my child do I believe best to start with? How will my child's success in overcoming this problem be foundational to my child overcoming his other struggles? Is there a main concern that I can think of that might be even more foundational, no matter how small, that I need to help my child overcome first?

If you have another major caregiver involved, you may want to do this exercise with that person. If so, brainstorm together to come up with one list of your combined main concerns or make individual lists and compare. Next, both of you individually pick the one main concern from your list that you feel is foundational to help your child overcome first. Come to an agreement about which main concern to help your child overcome first. The one you believe is foundational to helping your child overcome all of your main concerns in time.

Chastity

Chastity was being raised by her grandparents. Their main concerns were:

- Talking back
- Arguing
- Making excuses

- Not doing what she was supposed to do
- Whining
- Battles over homework
- Not wanting to get up for school

I asked Chastity's caregivers what instigated the problems they were describing, and they indicated that their granddaughter argued, talked back, made excuses and whined all in her attempt to delay or get out of doing what she was supposed to do. I asked them, "If she did what she was supposed to do right away, would she have many of the other problems?" They realized she likely wouldn't. They decided the main problem was Chasity not wanting to do what she was supposed to do.

Chastity's grandparents represent many people co-caregiving. They both loved Chastity and clearly wanted what was best for her; however, they totally disagreed on how to go about it. Her grandpa felt his wife was way too soft. The grandmother felt her husband was too hard on Chastity. When they made their lists of main concerns, they both agreed on the problems. This is what occurs with many couples in the process. This allowed them to focus on how to work together to help Chastity succeed in this area.

Every area of concern that you have for your child is important; however, focus your attention and energy on only one specific area of concern at a time. Which one specific main concern will be foundational to start with? Your identification of your answer to this question completes step one in defining your Expectation of Excellence.

Step 2: Define Your Specific Expectation

You will train your child to overcome the main concern you specified. Whether that concern is not doing what you tell him, throwing tantrums, aggressive behavior, academic struggles, shutting down, repeating over and over, lack of focus, or irresponsibility, you will help your child build the skills to overcome this problem forever.

Now that you have chosen to believe your child is capable, you will define an Expectation that you will train your child to meet consistently. Your loving relationship with your child will make your actions clear. First, specify how your child is responding to life in a maladaptive way. Then, envision how you'd like your child to respond. Have that image? That is exactly how you will train your child to respond, and it is absolutely possible that your child will learn to respond in that specific way.

Think of the specific response you will expect from your child. Now, "actionize" that response into a statement of a clear, specific Expectation. Here are some examples the families we are discussing came up with:

Grant's Co-parents:

> Main concern: Grant not listening to them
> Expectation: "Grant, you will do what we tell you to do the first time we tell you."

Simon's parents:

> Main concern: Fighting with him daily over the morning routine before school
> Expectation: "Simon, you will be in the car with your backpack by 7:15 am, fully dressed, wearing deodorant."

Jasmine's mom:

> Main concern: Tantrums in school almost daily
> Expectation: "Jasmine, you will not throw any tantrums at school."

Chastity's grandparents:

> Main concern: Not doing what she is supposed to be doing
> Expectation: "Chastity, you will do what we tell you to
> do right away."

Bill was being raised by a single mom. Let's add their example:
Bill's mom:

> Main concern: Bill hitting her
> Expectation: "Bill, you will use your words to communi-
> cate and not your actions."

Ambiguity must go. You must be clear in your mind about what you expect from your child so you can be fair in your Affirming Accountability. Besides, you don't want your smart warrior finding cracks in your Expectation. This expectation is too vague: "Charlotte, you will be nice from now on." That sounds kind; however, "be nice" can still leave you battling on too many fronts at once as you bounce from this to that trying to help your child "be nice."

Your child 12 and under, your concrete choice-and-consequence learner, needs specifics. You will be more effective and also empowered with measurable objectives. At the end of each day, it can be hard to quantify whether your child was "nice" that day. You essentially want to be able to measure your child's responses with *yes* and *no*. You can measure with a *yes* or *no*, "Did my child hit anyone today? Did my child hit his siblings today? Did my child throw a tantrum?

Did my child do what I told him right away? Did my child hit me?" The more clear, specific, and cut-and-dried you can be, the better it will be for training your child.

In the case of Bill's mom, her own language for her Expectation was, "Bill, you will use your words to communicate and not your actions." This was fine as Bill's mom would tell him this meant, "I will no longer accept you hitting me. If you hit me, kick me, or push me, you will be in big trouble." I would suggest, however, defining your Expectation in the most concise and precise manner possible. Words may have worked on you growing up. Are they working for your child? Think about how to define your Expectation in a way your child will understand. Bill's mom's was teaching him to use his words and not his hands when upset. Another potential variation of her Expectation could be, "You will control yourself and not hit."

Expectation & Faith

Set your Expectation based on belief in your child and her ability. Have faith in your child. Remember earlier in this section when you envisioned how you'd like your child to respond? That is the key for your child. In order to build your child up in the process of learning to build essential skills, you will challenge your child to Excellence. Excellence is not perfection. Excellence is your child's actions clearly showing her best effort. The cool thing is you will be hard on your child in a way that will build up your child based on your belief in her.

Let's use Grant as an example. The Expectation set for him is, "You will do what we tell you to do the first time we tell you." His caregivers first believed he was capable of achieving this goal. Once you believe your child to be capable of achieving your Expectation, you then have the opportunity to have faith that your child can achieve the positive expectation you have for him. Belief...then faith. Don't just think about your Expectation as stopping a behavior. Dream about it as your child fulfilling your hope. Instead of, "You will not hit," it's "From now on, you will control yourself regardless of how you feel." That is your clear, specific Expectation.

When you sit down with your child, you can communicate why you have set this expectation for her, such as, "I know you are capable of this; therefore, I'm going to hold you to this from now on. I will accept nothing less than your very best because I know what you can do. No longer will I tolerate any of the negative behavior because you are capable of controlling yourself each and every time. If you choose not to, you will be in big trouble."

Expectation Extrapolation

Your specific Expectation is there for your child, whether they are with you or not. Grant and Chastity had to meet their caregivers' clear, specific Expectation with their caregivers themselves. Jasmine had to meet her caregiver's Expectation at school. Whether your child is struggling around you or with others, she is accountable to your Expectation wherever they go. When you set your Expectation with your child, make sure you have the ability to get daily feedback concerning how your child met your Expectation. Hold her accountable accordingly.

Oxford

Oxford and his ex-wife, Patrice, couldn't stand each other. They were battling legally over custody of their son, Thomas. Thomas knew his parents didn't like each other, and this weighed heavily on his eight-year-old heart. Both parents currently split custody of Thomas. They were encouraged to shield Thomas from any vitriol. From there, his parents were encouraged to focus on empowering Thomas to stop having tantrums. What the other parent was or wasn't doing was out of their control. They individually had the opportunity to set an Expectation of Excellence with Thomas and empower him to develop self-control.

Oxford's main concern was Thomas' tantrums, which he largely displayed when he was not with his dad. Oxford's specific Expectation of Excellence was, "You will practice good ways of handling yourself when upset without tantrums." Oxford focused on empowering his son instead of blaming his ex-wife. He worked on getting daily reports when it was his turn for Thomas to be with him about how well Thomas achieved his

Expectation of Excellence. Oxford effectively praised his son when he met the Expectation to any degree and held him accountable to meeting the Expectation with Excellence when he did not.

Wax On. Wax Off.

In the 1984 release of the original "Karate Kid" movie, Ralph Macchio plays a bullied teen who ultimately learns karate from an unsuspected karate guru, "Mr. Miyagi" played by Pat Morita. Mr. Miyagi's unorthodox methods trained skills through hard work to achieve specific expectations. When "Daniel," Ralph Macchio's character, showed up early each morning for karate lessons, he was instructed to do a specific task in a specific way each day. One day he washed and waxed a lot full of antique cars, another day he painted a long fence and another he sanded a huge deck. In the infamous scene where Daniel is fed up with the laborious tasks on the evening of the third long day, Mr. Miyagi reveals that the specific actions Daniel used for each task trained him to perform an essential karate skill.

Now we challenge your child to work hard to transform. Your Expectation of Excellence raises the bar based on your belief in your child. Imagine the encouragement of your child hearing, "I believe in you." More importantly, imagine the power and positive sense of self when your child achieves the Expectation set for her with Excellence.

We know the behavior needs to change, but more importantly, your child's life, reputation, relationships, opportunities and safety need to improve. Daniel did not enjoy the hard work he endured in his training process; however, it unlocked potential he never knew he had...including two movie sequels. In your process of training your child to meet your specific Expectation, you are communicating through your actions, "I believe in what you are capable of." This will be a powerful prophecy your child will achieve as she builds essential life skills and unlocks her potential. Take time now to define your specific Expectation. In about eight words or less, write or verbalize the specific Expectation of Excellence you will empower your child to achieve.

Step 3: Recognize the Life Skill

Congratulations, you have completed steps one and two of defining your Expectation of Excellence for your child. You have identified your main concern. You have defined your specific Expectation for your child. You will now recognize the essential life skill or skills your child will build.

Helping your child overcome the problems he is having will undoubtedly bring relief to you, but this is not a selfish endeavor. You want your child to avoid the pain life will bring if he does not change course. Why is it important for your child to overcome the main concern you have for him? Think about this for a few seconds.

Tracy and Fred were concerned that they were being petty when the main concern they picked from their list was their son not getting out of bed and ready for school in the morning on his own. It was a battle each morning to get Zeek up for school, and Fred and Tracy were exhausted with this tedious routine. They had a hard time being on the same page in their caregiving before they came to my office; however, when they began discussing the main concerns they had for their son, they were surprised to find they were in almost complete agreement.

Fred and Tracy had another important revelation in this stage of creating their comprehensive Plan that many caregivers do, that the life skills behind the main concern they chose were not trivial at all. Tracy and Fred realized they truly wanted their son to develop responsibility. They knew Zeek was not being responsible in the way he handled himself in the mornings, and they were taking on a large part of the responsibility of getting him up and to school on time. They were trying to force their son to make it to school on time because they feared academic failure, problems with truancy and everyone being in trouble, including themselves.

Tracy and Fred agreed that helping Zeek become a responsible person was key to his future success. They decided to make Zeek fully responsible for getting up and to school on time. They even made it Zeek's responsibility to request any tools he needed for his success instead of trying to figure out for him how to get up. These changes empowered Zeek to fully own the responsibility of getting up and to school on time.

Fred and Tracy created a Plan to avoid micromanaging Zeek. They decided to put their energy into empowering a routine, giving encouragement, and applying Affirming Accountability in serious measure when Zeek did not meet the Expectation of "You will get up on your own and be at school on time." Fred and Tracy skillfully planned how to address all the potential problems Zeek might have and throw at them. Also, they focused on their purpose, their son becoming a responsible person, beyond their pain of training him to become one.

For Fred and Tracy, the opportunity to help their son build the essential life skill of responsibility was worth the risks they would face in the process. They decided to face their fears of Zeek failing, getting in trouble with the law and them being in trouble for Zeek's truancy. They allowed the hope of Zeek becoming a responsible young man to guide their actions when they were tempted to give in to their fears and all the pressures.

Focusing on the essential life skills we are determined to help our child build will guide our actions above the pain and pressures. Let's reexamine the examples from earlier in this part of the book to discover the essential life skills these caregivers focused on:

Grant's caregivers:

Main concern: Grant not listening to them
Expectation: "Grant, you will do what we tell you to do the first time we tell you."
Life Skills: Respect, Responsibility

Bill's mom:

Main concern: Bill hitting her

Expectation: "Bill, you will use your words to communicate and not your actions."

Life Skills: Self-control, Healthy Communication, Boundaries, Respect

Jasmine's mom:

Main concern: Tantrums in school almost daily

Expectation: "Jasmine, you will not throw any tantrums at school."

Life Skills: Self-control, Respect, Responsibility, Self-Discipline

Chastity's grandparents:

Main concern: Not doing what she is supposed to be doing

Expectation: "Chastity, you will do what we tell you to do right away."

Life Skills: Respect, Responsibility, Self-Discipline

Simon's parents:

Main concern: Fighting with him daily over the morning routine before school

Expectation: "Simon, you will be in the car with your backpack by 7:15 am, fully dressed, wearing deodorant ."

Life Skill: Responsibility

Now we get to identify your "purpose beyond the pain." Which essential life skill or skills will you help your child build? Your purpose will guide your child in building life skills that you believe are essential to his safety, success and happiness.

Your Expectation of Excellence

You have defined your main concern, stated your specific Expectation and identified the life skills your child will build internally. These elements create your Expectation of Excellence because you will accept nothing less. When you are tempted to let go of your Expectation or accept something less than Excellence, keep in mind your hopes for your child. These are rooted in faith in God and the essential life skills you are helping your child build. Hold on to both when you feel exhausted, afraid, confused or are tempted to doubt.

When you begin the process, after you have put together your comprehensive Plan, remain consistent in empowering your child to achieve your Expectation of Excellence. When your child achieves your Expectation of Excellence, he will feel good inside. Remain focused on your purpose beyond the pain until they do so. Your child can achieve Excellence, unlocking your child's greatest potential. Now let's look at how to motivate your 12 and under, choice-and-consequence learner to push his energy into Excellence through Affirming Accountability—the A in L.E.A.P.

CHAPTER 9

AFFIRMING ACCOUNTABILITY

Healthy Power

"For the kingdom of God is not a matter of talk but of power."
—1 Corinthians 4:20

Healthy power will be your child building the understanding and internal desire to pour her energy consistently into beneficial choices. Your 12 and under, choice-and-consequence learner, is characterologically, morally, and neurophysiologically designed by the Creator to need your help to develop her power. Children know deep down that their maladaptive behavior is wrong and not good for them. This is why they seem so remorseful after they've done something unhealthy, but then repeat the behavior. They sometimes even repeat the behavior right away, because their impulses in the moment are stronger than their power to overcome them. Affirming Accountability in the context of a loving relationship is the key to empower your child to redirect her energy away from maladaptive choices and into building her healthy power.

Affirming Accountability Is...

Affirming Accountability is faith and courage in action supporting your hopes for your child. You are embracing the idea that your child is capable. You've identified your Expectation of Excellence. Now, prepare to effectively empower your child with Affirming Accountability.

> Affirming: "I believe you are capable of meeting this specific Expectation of Excellence."

> Accountability: I will act to reinforce my belief in my child and what my child is capable of.

> Affirming: "This is what you did well. What do I expect of you though? I know you are capable of Excellence, and I will accept nothing less. I love you."

Affirming Accountability is action. Excessive talking, yelling, screaming, cajoling, rewarding and even medication are not effective in helping a child develop healthy power. Healthy power in your 12 and under, choice-and-consequence learner is developed through effectively connecting choice to consequence in the context of a loving relationship.

Affirming is communicating your belief in your child through words. You will constantly affirm your child. When you think, pray and speak like you know your child can achieve with Excellence the positive Expectation you set, this will build up your child. It's important that Affirming be continual. Even when your child fails, you can Affirm your child. You can Affirm your belief in her ability and any improvements, even if small.

Accountability is communicating your belief in your child through actions. Accountability is holding your child fully responsible to use her ingenuity, intelligence, and ability to achieve the positive Expectation you set for her. Accountability is firm and effective discipline in the context of a loving relationship. I call this lovingly firm discipline. When your child pushes her energy away from non-beneficial choices and into beneficial choices, the fruit of her labor will build her up on the inside.

Our Children Need Affirming Accountability

Your child has an inner battle going on. Her impulses, momentary desires, temporary rewards and habits are just too powerful for her to overcome in and of themselves. The loving bond you have with your child is the most effective proponent of healthy power, while lovingly firm discipline is the most effective deterrent of unhealthy choices. Your child needs both in effective measure. At times, effective measure is saying no and sticking to it. Other times, effective measure will be natural and imposed consequences of sufficient type and degree to matter to your child.

Our job as caregivers is to empower our child daily with our proponent, Love, and deterrent, Affirming Accountability. The power of Love includes Affirming Accountability and is stronger than our child's impulses, maladaptive rewards and poor habits. When your child is empowered with both, in effective measure specific to her, your child will have what she needs to win her internal battle.

I hear many caregivers express, "I wish my child would just do what he needs to do. I don't want to have to threaten consequences to get my child to do the right thing," or "I didn't have to be threatened with consequences to do the right thing growing up." I empathize with you. I wish talking, encouraging and rewarding our choice-and-consequence learners were primary means to helping them build their healthy power. For children operating primarily in line with the compliant or slow-to-warm-up temperament, sure, these milder measures are effective. For the child compelling you to read this book, however, Affirming without Accountability is powerless.

What's Important *For* Connected To What's Important *In*

It's all connected, my wife Heather often says. Well, indeed it is, Heather, indeed it is. Our kids usually do not care about what's important for their lives. All kids do, however, have privileges that are important in their lives. To effectively empower your child, your Affirming Accountability must connect what's important FOR your child's life to what's important IN your child's life. A child can walk by the overflowing trash bin. Adults can look with incredulity at the spectacle wondering, "Did he not see that?" The truth is, your child didn't see it. The overflowing trash is on your radar because you are directly connected to all the consequences of not taking it out. Your child is not. Your child can literally walk up to the trash bin, add something to the overflowing pile and walk away without it even registering. The trash bin will not be on your child's radar until you directly connect taking care of the trash with something important to your child.

I loved Saturday morning cartoons growing up. My mom indicated my chores all had to be done Saturday morning, excellently, before I could watch any of my shows. Since my shows were extremely important to me, I got up early and did my chores. My mom quickly taught me that trying to get by with less than doing the job well would cost me my shows. After a while, I was in a routine of getting up on my own and getting my chores done well so I could watch my shows. I never realized that my mom had implemented with me when I was growing up what I now call Affirming Accountability...until about the time I started writing this book. Mom, I'm shouting out posthumous credit for your wisdom.

I couldn't have cared less about the sweeping, cleaning and dusting I did as a kid. Who cared about a dust bunny? I wanted to watch Bugs Bunny! Dirt in the corners of the room...pleeeeease! What dirt? My shows though? Now those were important. Your Expectation of Excellence and the corresponding life skills you want your child to develop are important FOR your child's life. What's important IN your child's life? Affirming Accountability effectively connects the two.

Overcoming Anxiety & Poor Image
with Affirming Accountability

I hate myself! I'm scared! The monster is going to get me! Someone will break in and kill me! I'm terrible! I'm bad! I wish I wasn't born! I'm stupid! I want to do good, but I can't! The storm will eat me!

Hearing your child make comments such as these is heartbreaking. We don't want our children to feel bad about themselves or their lives. We don't want them to live in pain and fear. We desperately want our children to be happy and at peace. Many caregivers also don't want to live with a guilt deep down inside that their child's struggles are their fault. Let's understand why many children express the above-mentioned feelings and fears. In order to do so effectively, let's keep in the forefront of our minds where our children are developmentally. Children 12 and under are primarily concrete, black-and-white, choice-and-consequence thinkers.

Due to both their concrete and magical thinking, children equate in their own minds bad or maladaptive behavior to: 1) being bad themselves or something being wrong with them; or 2) something bad inevitably happening. These are ubiquitous yet unrecognized manifestations of a child's internal struggle with his choices.

First, children equate bad or maladaptive behavior to being bad themselves or something being wrong with them. Even if the behavior is not "bad" per se, a child knows deep down what he is capable of and when he is not reaching his potential. Sometimes a child will exclaim something like, "I'm stupid!" or "I can't!" to pull an adult into doing for him what he knows deep down he can and should do for himself. Sometimes kids will criticize themselves because they know that when they do, adults will soften and console their emotions instead of confronting their behavior. At other times, the child is simply yet profoundly expressing the truth…"I am hurting because time and time again I lose the inner battle against my impulses in the moment."

Secondly, intensive fears and anxieties for a child 12 and under can be a result of concrete and imaginative thinking as a result of poor choices. Kids know their behavior is wrong or not okay. They feel bad, yet also feel they don't have the strength to overcome their impulses. The height of the impulse leads to a choice followed by fear afterward. The fear can be rational, such as getting in trouble. The fear can also be magical, in the form of a child fearing supernatural reprisal. Magical thinking can cause a child who is angry to think, "I wish mommy would get hit by a truck" only to fear later that the "wish" will come true. In this, a child might cling to mom, which appears as separation anxiety, for fear that something bad will happen to her. Also, because of the child's behavior, the child may fear supernatural reprisal in the form of something terrible happening to those she loves.

Post-poor choice worries can intensify and begin to manifest as symptoms of anxiety in general. Children 12 and under can begin to believe of their own accord that their maladaptive behavior will cause God, the universe, or the babayka to punish them, even though none of this is true. They can begin to fear the dark, fear being alone, or fear something terrible will happen to them in the form of a reprisal from monsters, storms, intruders, illness and accidents, to name most but not all.

The root of unhealthy anxiety is in our thinking processes. If you have a child struggling with maladaptive choices and anxiety of some kind, you want to help her with both. Continue to Affirm her feelings and provide lovingly firm Accountability for her choices. A child can feel angry, scared, worried and have other challenging feelings we Affirm by accepting and providing her healthy means to process her feelings. Your child does not benefit, though, from expressing her feelings through a lack of self-control. Your child doesn't have to scream, hit something or someone, or necessarily have extra measures to go to a certain place when upset. Sure, a place for time away can be helpful, yet we are missing the point.

What your child needs is Affirmation of his feelings through absolute acceptance combined with resolute Accountability for repeated poor choices. This Affirms in our children that feelings are acceptable. Whatever the feeling might be, the child needs to know those feelings are legitimate. A child can feel whatever he feels, yet he must choose to control himself despite his feelings. Despite what you've witnessed, your child is likely capable of self-control; but this skill is undeveloped and unrefined. Empowering children to make better choices powerfully helps them to feel better about their decisions. This in turn causes them to feel good about themselves.

Continue to Affirm your child verbally with the reality of her poor choices not causing her to be a bad person and that she will not cause some supernatural hurt to herself or someone else. Also, empower her with Accountability to help your child make better decisions. This can help children feel better about their behavior, often quieting anxiety fueled by magical thinking. When children 12 and under are doing well, they can often feel more emotionally at ease because right choices lead to right feelings.

97% to 98% Effectiveness Wins the Day

You are already doing at least 70% to 80% of the Most Effective Actions to help your child succeed; unfortunately, it's not enough. To empower your child to win her inner battle, you must consistently operate in the 97% to 98% range. When you complete and implement your comprehensive Plan, with each element of L.E.A.P. tailored to your child, you will be able to operate daily in the 97% to 98% range of the Most Effective Actions to help your child succeed. Your Affirming Accountability built on the foundation of the loving relationship will be one of the strongest elements empowering your child's success.

Many of you are already giving consequences on a regular basis; however, you are likely operating overall in the 70% to 80% range of the Most Effective Actions. Tweaks are needed to get you to the 97% to 98% range. Maybe confusion hindered you in the past. Confusion hinders many caregivers because they aren't sure what's wrong with their child and what to do about it.

Many caregivers, especially females, believe they are being extremely firm with their child; but their child in truth doesn't take their discipline seriously most of the time. Sometimes caregivers are hindered by fear, guilt, other people or patterns of enabling. Maybe you've worried that firm Accountability for your child's behavior might be unfair or make him worse. Affirming Accountability will empower your child to do and feel better about himself, his life, and his ability. What can you tweak to make sure you are moving from the 70% to 80% range of the Most Effective Actions to the 97% to 98% range with your Affirming Accountability?

For most this means putting together a comprehensive Plan, including sound Affirming Accountability. Let me give you an example. A dad and I discussed Affirming Accountability in my office. We began brainstorming about specific Accountability measures that would likely be effective for his stepson. We identified an accountability measure used in the past when his child disobeyed, he and his wife would take a specific privilege...sort of, but not really.

The dad and I discussed that just *threatening* to take one privilege or another is not powerful enough; follow-through is key. Affirming Accountability must be a part of the comprehensive process to train your child to succeed in a way she hasn't to this point. A comprehensive process includes reinforcing the loving bond, discipline, routine, proactive prevention measures, taking out the "fluff," picking your battles, noticing and Affirming any improvement, and having a Plan for your worst-case scenario. A comprehensive Plan is the effective process that moves you from "fix the problem," to "empower your child to overcome the problem." Your focus and energy must be on the process, not the problem. An effective process will help your child build the skills from the inside out to overcome the problem for good while gaining strength and confidence.

By the time the dad and I finished our discussion, he had the beginnings of a sound process. We reviewed his Expectation of Excellence:

"You will do what you are told right away." We discussed time out on his son's bed, a more effective time out process shared in the Resource Guide, and training the child to accept that process. The dad began to visualize carefully selecting the polite commands he gave his son, as each polite command enacted his Expectation of Excellence. We discussed he and his wife taking out the "fluff" of reminding, a lot of talking, and rewarding. We strategized how they could incorporate routine to empower what they needed their son to do. We focused on how he could effectively reinforce his Expectations with specific measures that connected what was important FOR his child's life to what is important IN his child's life. We reinforced the importance of recognizing and Affirming all improvements along the way. By the end of the session, the work the dad accomplished creating his Plan brought him and his wife much closer to the 97% to 98% range of effectiveness. He committed to going home and working with his wife to complete their Plan.

Affirming Accountability by Design

If needed, the Resource Guide and Workbook will help you design your comprehensive Plan. In order to tailor your Plan to the needs of your child, pick and choose which of the highly effective strategies will be most effective to empower your child's success. Trust yourself. God gave you the child in your care for a reason.

Some of you have been waiting to get to the "what to do part" only to read, "Use the Resource Guide & Workbook." This is only because I want your utmost success. You get to put together your comprehensive and highly effective Plan for Affirming Accountability with the resources provided. You are the expert on your child. What will work in empowering your child to transform? Only you will know the specifics.

The L.E.A.P. process works when you work it. The tools are effective when you tailor your Plan to implement Affirming Accountability according to what is Most Effective for you and your child. Use the Resource

Guide to accentuate your current effective strategies. Use the Workbook to fully prepare your Plan. Doing this on the front end will save you time and help you avoid land mines that will destroy the results of the unprepared.

Put your Plan together completely before you implement it. Why is this important? You are about to enter the family version of the reality show *Survivor!* Trust me, you can't afford to get voted off the island. Once you implement your process, you have to outwit, outlast and outplay until your child surrenders to your will and achieves Excellence.

Our children are designed to need Affirming Accountability. Affirm your belief in your child up front. Consistently hold your child Accountable to meet your Expectation of Excellence. Affirm what they did well in the process and repeat. Make sure your Affirming Accountability accomplishes the following:

1. It should be part of your comprehensive Plan.
2. It should be in effective measure with your specific child.
3. It must connect what's important FOR your child's life to what's important IN your child's life.

Lovingly firm discipline will break the will but never crush the spirit. When your child's will that is pointed in an unhealthy direction is broken, she will pour her energy in a healthy direction. Your child will reap the rewards of internal strength, confidence, better relationships, peace of mind and good feelings about herself and her future. Outwit, outlast and outplay until your child gets there…you must Persevere, which leads us to the final letter in the L.E.A.P. process.

CHAPTER 10

PERSEVERANCE

"The end of your rope is just the beginning of
perseverance."

—AJ McMahan

This step is essential once your Plan is complete. You have put the
foundation of the loving relationship in place. You have identified
the one main concern you want to help your child overcome first.
You have set your Expectation of Excellence. You have identified the 70%
to 80% of your Most Effective Actions that you already have in place.
Using the Resource Guide and Workbook, you have tweaked your Plan
to the 97% to 98% range of the Most Effective Actions on a daily basis to
help your child succeed.

Now you are ready to Persevere as you put your Plan in place to empower your child to transform. Here are a few essential elements:

1. Continue to connect relationally during your process.
2. What you accept is what you get. Accept nothing less than
   Excellence.
3. Discuss your Accountability ideas along the way with a lovingly
   firm caregiver.

Take the L.E.A.P.

Launch your Plan by sitting down with your child and explaining briefly your specific Expectation of Excellence going forward. Make sure your child knows exactly what you expect and that you love and believe in your child.

Take ownership of mistakes you've made so far and commit before your child to correct him for his own well-being. Be careful not to confuse this with taking ownership *for* your child's problems—this is *not* that. Your child could have exactly the same problems even if he had a virtually problem-free life up to this point.

Then implement your Plan.

Pattern 1, Pattern 2. Ha! I'll Show You!

This is what's going to happen after your succinct conversation. Your child won't believe you will stick to holding her to your Expectation of Excellence or will secretly have a "we'll see" attitude. As you implement your Plan, one of two patterns will occur:

> Pattern 1: Your child will immediately begin to rebel. He will get much worse before he gets better. He will either challenge you stronger than ever or be passive-aggressive. Passive aggressiveness is defined by Wikipedia as the "indirect expression of hostility, such as through procrastination, sarcasm, hostile jokes, stubbornness, resentment, sullenness, or deliberate or repeated failure to accomplish requested tasks for which one is (often explicitly) responsible." Yeah, that's going to happen.

> Pattern 2: Your child will almost immediately improve. She will begin to do much better, then after a relatively brief period of time, she will go into Pattern 1.

Pattern 1 tests your resolve immediately. Persevere. You have a Plan. You are capable. This will work. If your child follows Pattern 2, you may feel amazed and excited about the positive change you see in your child. You may feel that what you are doing is "working" and that I'm a genius... until everything goes downhill. The problems will come back, likely with a vengeance!

Caregivers who are not prepared for Pattern 2 may think this is like previous occurrences when you've tried a new method where changes occurred but didn't last. I assure you this will not be the case with this program if you will simply Persevere with your Plan.

Rough Patches

You are now helping your child build, not just behave. Internal character strength is what your child is building. This takes time. Whether it be foundational self-discipline or self-control in forms of respect or responsibility, you are helping your child build lifelong skills. During this process, your child will go through what I call "rough patches."

During the L.E.A.P. process, your child will go back and forth from rough patches to peace patches like an accordion. Rough patches are the times when your child will display the same old behavior. A rough patch can last minutes or weeks. Peace patches are when your child will show improvement and be the sweet, wonderful, progressing child you know she is.

The back and forth accordion-like process will last on average from four to nine months, with incremental gains. I've never seen a child transform without rough patches. I've seen near exasperation for caregivers when the rough patches last for weeks...which happens. Be prepared. Rough patches are normal. Remain consistent with your Plan and Persevere.

Your child must surrender to your lovingly firm boundaries and discipline. You cannot be the one to give in! Even if you have to fake it until you make it, do so in love. You're fully engaged in the family version of *Survivor!*, remember? Pray and hang in there! Your child must gain confidence in your consistency as you Persevere. Persevere until you see your child direct her energy inward, choose to meet your Expectation with only Excellence, and be proud of herself.

When following this process while trusting in God and believing in yourself and your child, you will see your child work through the rough patches. Incrementally and perhaps even unnoticeably at first, the rough patches will become a little less intense and the peace patches will become a little more prominent. One day you'll look up and say to yourself or your partner, "When was the last time our child had such-and-such problem?" When the transformation finally takes hold in your child, you will see his ability to consistently shine.

We build physical muscle from stressing muscles in healthy ways. The muscles break down from the stress and then grow stronger as a result. Your child is building character muscles. Persevere through the rough patches with love and consistency, and your child will likely grow strong enough not just to behave better but transform.

This Is Not Working!!!

Janet came back to my office about three weeks into the process of following the Plan we created with L.E.A.P. to help her child succeed. Over and over again, I've seen L.E.A.P. work consistently with families, but Janet rattled me.

"It's not working!!" she exclaimed.

"Tell me what's going on," I replied, purposely remaining calm. Janet had a strong foundation of a loving relationship with her six-year-old son. Her Expectation of Excellence was for Sam to do what he was told the first time. With a process, not problem focus, I shifted the conversation to allow Janet to verify her consistency with Affirming Accountability, which she did. "How is Sam responding to your Plan?" I asked.

"That's the problem," Janet exclaimed. "He is saying all types of horrible things to me like 'You're a mean mommy' or 'You're a nasty mommy!' He gets so angry and grunts or says these terrible things to me!"

"How is he doing when it comes to doing what you tell him the first time?" I calmy asked.

Thoughtfully, Janet replied, "Actually, he's doing much better with that. He's doing what I tell him the first time almost every time now. It's just that he says these mean things to me in the process." I exhaled imperceptibly with relief.

What Janet experienced is normal, and you may find yourself in a similar situation. Your child will be unhappy about your consistent Affirming Accountability and Perseverance with the process. Your child will probably let you know she is unhappy. Also, your child still has other issues of concern outside of your Expectation of Excellence. For now, anything beyond your Expectation of Excellence that doesn't absolutely have to be addressed can wait.

I advised Janet to continue focusing on Sam doing what she told him the first time. Once she was confident that his gains in this area were solidified, then she could move on to adding the next Expectation of Excellence which would be expressed to Sam as, "You will do what I tell you without any back talk."

You have limited time, energy, and resources. Each and every time you and your child cross your Expectation of Excellence, you must act. You cannot afford any cracks in your consistency with Affirming Accountability when it comes to your Expectation of Excellence. Cracks in consistency produce unintentional reinforcement for unhealthy choices and encourage stubbornness. You do not want your child thinking that, if they wear you down, you might give in. You want your child to learn that putting energy into trying to get over, under, around or through you won't work. The only way that's successful is when they push their energy WITH you. You must reserve as much of your limited time, energy and resources as possible to act without fail to reinforce your Expectation of Excellence until your child succeeds.

Focusing on helping your child win one major battle at a time is the most effective way to "pick your battles" while helping your child win his. This "one at a time" specific building process will help your child focus and experience success in this one specific area. Your child will also build confidence in himself by repeatedly reaching the new bar that you've set. Once your child consistently demonstrates gains with your Expectation of Excellence, only then should you move on to the next foundational skill you want to build in your child.

When Sam became consistent with doing what Janet told him the first time, she added the next Expectation of, "You will obey without back talk." She remained focused that once Sam was doing what she told him consistently that it would be easier for her to train him to obey without back talk. This is when she would effectively help Sam stop the unsettling verbalizations.

Help your child win one major battle at a time against his impulses in order to produce new actions and solidify them into habits, which will put your child on a solid path to building character. Then add another and another.

Bittersweet

At first, your child's battle against her impulses will still rage strong. She knows the sweet taste of getting her way sometimes, or getting out of what she doesn't want, or giving in to her impulses and getting the tons of hidden rewards she finds worthwhile—and she's not going to easily relinquish them. Very firm consequences that are not too hard, but definitely not too soft, in the context of a loving relationship connect a "bitter taste" in your child's mind between the non-beneficial choice and the outcome. In her heart, your child will not connect the consequences with a bitter taste about her relationship with you, because you have made sure that she knows that you love her and knows that anyone involved in lovingly firm discipline loves her. Remember, it's not about whether the adults know they love the child. This is not enough. Your child has to know in her heart that the disciplinarian loves her. When she does, your child is not confused about the firm yet fair consequences that you have told her will inevitably result for certain choices. In time, your child will make a direct connection between the choice and the consequence needed to help her redirect her energy positively.

Persist with Love

No matter what lovingly firm discipline you choose, it will take time for this discipline to be effective. We do not burn our children when they make bad choices. This is why discipline cannot be equated to the proverbial "hot stove." A burn from a hot stove is so intense, we may need to experience that only once to be cautious forever. There is no discipline that equates to the pain of us burning ourselves from touching a hot stove, nor should there ever be. Discipline must be consistent, measured pain—a pain that says, "I love you. I believe in your ability to do better, so in the most firm way I believe is fair, I will hold you accountable. I do not do this to harm you. I do this to help you to see the importance of changing this behavior that is destroying you. I cannot make you change, but I also won't stand by and do nothing while you continue making choices that kill your hopes, dreams and potential without even knowing it."

My kids will tell you that I give very firm spankings, and they hurt. My kids cry, hurt, and still love me. I do not give spankings because I want to hurt them. I give spankings because sometimes that's what's needed to really help my child think about the unhealthy choice and think twice about making it. I know that sometimes, spankings are the most effective way to get through to my child. Spankings might be the most effective way for you to get through to your child at times. Even so, when we decide to spank and make it effective by hurting our children appropriately in love and with Godly wisdom when they cross specific boundaries we have set, we do not bring pain equivalent to burning them or the like.

Our lovingly firm discipline will not be a one-and-done experience, so we must persist...but we persist with love. No matter what discipline we use for our kids, there is something about the loving relationship that discipline can never equate to. A teen whose mom got so desperate for him to get up for school splashed him with water as he lay in bed, and on one occasion when he locked the door, she even went on the roof and crawled through his window to wake him up. I'm not advocating for these methods. What I want you to know is that the teen finally decided to get up on his own and go to school every day. He decided to change not because of the water, the roof or any of his mom's other desperate efforts, but because as the teen told me about his mom, "She never stopped loving me, and I got tired of seeing her hurt."

Keep Chasing the Heart

No matter what you do, never stop chasing your child's heart. If you are so frustrated with your child that you can hardly be around him, accept that. You might even need to speak the truth in love with your child: "I love you, and I always will; but I don't like you right now. Your behavior drives me crazy, and I want to scream and run away. I won't, though, because I love you. Because I love you, I'm going to punish you. What did you do that I told you I will not tolerate? (The child answers). Right. You crossed that line, so here are your consequences."

Find your own way to love your child through your frustration. Know that loving your child means stepping up your game with discipline. It means loving your 12 and under child enough to embrace the truth about spanking and doing it if you need to. Loving your child means spending time with him at times that make sense like dinner, being there for school programs and other important events, and even that one minute of focused attention before bed. Zig Ziglar said, "How do kids spell love? T-I-M-E."

Our Child's Behavior Dictates Our Response

One child may get spankings, a lot of them, while another child may not. Our child's behavior dictates our response. Embrace the truth with yourself and your children that you love them enough to give them what they need. If a child, any child, breaks the family law, he will be disciplined according to his temperament and needs. That's the way of it. If one child breaks the law and the others do not, each child should receive the due consequences for his actions. Remember the word *consequences* relates to appropriate outcomes of a choice, not just punishment. Don't feel guilty if one child spends the day enjoying screens and having fun while the other spends all day in his room. Decide what's fair for each child and, to the best of your ability, respond accordingly.

Persevering with Spanking

Spanking appropriately is challenging. It takes skill to spank effectively. We have to learn how to spank in the "goldilocks zone," not too hard and not too soft. This takes work, effort and practice. As a caregiver I've made mistakes in judgment and errors in discipline and so will you. The key is the heart. The key is to own mistakes, apologize for them when appropriate and always learn from them. We must not let our mistakes cause us to be fueled with guilt that keeps us from learning and being the most effective caregiver we can be even when disciplining our kids. I did not make mistakes as a caregiver to try to hurt my children. I made these mistakes because I'm human. We will make mistakes.

The key is to put our child's best interest at the forefront. If you've made mistakes in disciplining your child, don't let this stop you from becoming skillful in discipline. Give Affirming Accountability according to your child's needs, not your feelings, fears, or past. I cannot change that some have and will beat children while saying this is for the child's best interest. These selfish, aggressive actions are not appropriate spankings.

These are malevolent rage in disguise and have nothing to do with appropriate spankings. I'm sorry for those of you that have endured a person in power taking his anger and aggression out on you.

As caregivers, our kids need us to move past our fear, hurt, worry and misgivings to embrace the truth about appropriate spankings. Our children need us to learn how to give effective and appropriate spankings in the "goldilocks zone" for our specific child. Details to help you if you decide to have spanking in your Affirming Accountability tool belt are found in the Resource Guide in the section called "Spanking." If your child fusses at you, yells at you, argues with you, fake cries, or gets angry with you during your spanking, these are signs that your spanking is not effective. Children do not need to be spanked for "every little thing." Sometimes, however, firm, effective and appropriate spankings can get through when milder measures can't. Appropriate spankings can be positively empowering to children when done in the effective measure, in effective ways, at wise times.

Always Persevere

Continue chasing after the heart of your child, regardless of how you feel or what she does. This can be difficult when your heart is hurt and broken. God is the only one who can heal our hearts and give us the courage and fortitude to Persevere in loving ways despite the hurt someone else is causing. Try not to take the words and actions of your struggling child personally. Try not to get caught up in blame for yourself or someone else. Remember what's most important. Ask God for what you need and Persevere.

Do not enable your child because this is not the loving path of Perseverance. Empower your child even if it hurts, focusing in hope on the larger goal. Trust God with your child, and act in line with what's most effective to help your child succeed. Tweak when necessary and Persevere with your Plan. Persevere through the doubters, through the rough patches, and even while the other concerns beyond your one major battle persist. Persevere until your child triumphs over his unhealthy impulse, his bad habit, his maladaptive choice. God will not fail you. You will not fail.

CPSIA information can be obtained
at www.ICGtesting.com
Printed in the USA
JSHW031913210222
23172JS00006B/157